BEYOND RELIGION

TENZIN GYATSO, His Holiness the Fourteenth Dalai Lama, is the spiritual leader of the Tibetan people. His tireless efforts on behalf of human rights and world peace have brought him international recognition. He is the recipient of the Raoul Wallenberg Congressional Human Rights Award, the Albert Schweitzer Humanitarian Award, the Congressional Gold Medal, and the Nobel Peace Prize.

Praise for *Beyond Religion*

"An impressive guide for teaching religious tolerance and respect to readers of all ages." —*Kirkus Reviews*

"The Dalai Lama's searchlight intelligence, wisdom, humor, humility, and hope make reading this inspiring crystallization of a lifetime of inquiry and reflection feel like the first step to answering His Holiness' core question for each of us, 'What can I contribute to the betterment of humanity?'" —*Booklist*

"A wise, humane book ... an incisive statement on ways to bring peace to a suffering world." —*Publishers Weekly*

HIS HOLINESS THE DALAI LAMA

BEYOND RELIGION

Ethics for a Whole World

HARPER element

First published in the US in 2011 by Houghton Mifflin Harcourt

First published in India in hardback in India
by HarperCollins *Publishers* in 2012

HarperCollins Publishers India, Cyber City, Building 10-A, Gurugram,
Haryana-122002, India
www.harpercollins.co.in

First published in paperback in 2014 by Harper Element
an imprint of HarperCollins *Publishers*

This edition published in 2015 by Harper Element

8 10 9 7

P-ISBN: 978-93-5136-080-3
E-ISBN: 978-93-5136-158-9

Book design by Melissa Lotfy

Printed and bound at
MicroPrints India, New Delhi

MIX
Paper
FSC FSC® C218906

This product is made of FSC®-certified and other controlled material.

HarperCollins Publishers, Macken House, 39/40 Mayor Street
Upper, Dublin 1, D01 C9W8, Ireland

Acknowledgments

In the writing of this book, I have been fortunate to have been assisted by the same editorial team that worked on my previous book, *Ethics for the New Millennium,* with the addition of one or two others. I would therefore like to acknowledge with gratitude the efforts of the concerned members of my Private Office, the invaluable help of my long-time translator, Thupten Jinpa Langri, and the editorial attention of Alexander Norman and his associate George FitzHerbert.

It is my sincere hope that what is written here may contribute, in however small a way, to building a more compassionate and more peaceful world. Of course we are not going to change the world overnight. And we will not change it with a short treatise such as this one. Change will come gradually through increased awareness, and awareness will only come with education. If the reader finds anything written here to be of benefit, then our endeavors will have been well rewarded. A reader who finds no such benefit should not feel any awkwardness about setting this book aside.

The Dalai Lama

Dharamsala, 2nd June 2011

Contents

Introduction

I am an old man now. I was born in 1935 in a small village in northeastern Tibet. For reasons beyond my control, I have lived most of my adult life as a stateless refugee in India, which has been my second home for over fifty years. I often joke that I am India's longest-staying guest. In common with other people of my age, I have witnessed many of the dramatic events that have shaped the world we live in. Since the late 1960s, I have also traveled a great deal, and had the honor to meet people from many different backgrounds: not just presidents and prime ministers, kings and queens, and leaders from all the world's great religious traditions, but also a great number of ordinary people from all walks of life.

Looking back over the past decades, I find many reasons to rejoice. Through advances in medical science, deadly diseases have been eradicated. Millions of people have been lifted from poverty and have gained access to modern education and health care. We have a universal declaration of human rights, and awareness of the importance of such rights has grown tremendously. As a result, the ideals of freedom and democracy have spread around the world, and there is increasing recognition of the oneness of humanity. There is also growing awareness of the importance of a healthy environment. In very many ways, the last half-century or so has been one of progress and positive change.

At the same time, despite tremendous advances in so many fields, there is still great suffering, and humanity continues to face enormous difficulties and problems. While in the more affluent parts of the world people enjoy lifestyles of high consumption, there remain countless millions whose basic needs are not met. With the end of the Cold War, the threat of global nuclear destruction has receded, but many continue to endure the sufferings and tragedy of armed conflict. In many areas, too, people are having to deal with environmental problems and, with these, threats to their livelihood and worse. At the same time, many others are struggling to get by in the face of inequality, corruption, and injustice.

These problems are not limited to the developing world. In the richer countries, too, there are many difficulties, including widespread social problems: alcoholism, drug abuse, domestic violence, family breakdown. People are worried about their children, about their education and what the world holds in store for them. Now, too, we have to recognize the possibility that human activity is damaging our planet beyond a point of no return, a threat which creates further fear. And all the pressures of modern life bring with them stress, anxiety, depression, and, increasingly, loneliness. As a result, everywhere I go, people are complaining. Even I find myself complaining from time to time!

It is clear that something is seriously lacking in the way we humans are going about things. But what is it that we lack? The fundamental problem, I believe, is that at every level we are giving too much attention to the external, material aspects of life while neglecting moral ethics and inner values.

By inner values I mean the qualities that we all appreciate in others, and toward which we all have a natural instinct, bequeathed by our biological nature as animals that survive and thrive only in an environment of concern, affection, and warm-heartedness—or in a single word, compassion. The essence of compassion is a desire to alleviate the suffering of others and to promote their well-being. This is the spiritual principle from which all other positive inner values emerge. We all appreciate in others the inner qualities of kindness, patience, tolerance, forgiveness, and generosity, and in the same way we are all averse to displays of greed, malice, hatred, and bigotry. So actively promoting the positive inner qualities of the human heart that arise from our core disposition toward compassion, and learning to combat our more destructive propensities, will be appreciated by all. And the first beneficiaries of such a strengthening of our inner values will, no doubt, be ourselves. Our inner lives are something we ignore at our own peril, and many of the greatest problems we face in today's world are the result of such neglect.

Not long ago I visited Orissa, a region in eastern India. The poverty in this part of the country, especially among tribal people, has recently led to growing conflict and insurgency. I met with a member of parliament from the region and discussed these issues. From him I gathered that there are a number of legal mechanisms and well-funded government projects already in place aimed at protecting the rights of tribal people and even giving them material assistance. The problem, he said, was that because of corruption these programs were not benefiting those they were intended to help. When such projects are subverted by dishonesty, inefficiency, and irresponsibility on the part of those charged with implementing them, they become worthless.

This example shows very clearly that even when a system is sound, its effectiveness depends on the way it is *used*. Ultimately, any system, any set of laws or procedures, can only be as effective as the individuals responsible for its implementation. If, owing to failures of personal integrity, a good system is misused, it can easily become a source of harm rather than a source of benefit. This is a general truth which applies to all fields of human activity, even religion. Though religion certainly has the potential to help people lead meaningful and happy lives, it too, when misused, can become a source of conflict and division. Similarly, in the fields of commerce and finance, the systems themselves may be sound, but if the people using them are unscrupulous and driven by self-serving greed, the benefits of those systems will be undermined. Unfortunately, we see this happening in many kinds of human activities: even in international sports, where corruption threatens the very notion of fair play.

Of course, many discerning people are aware of these problems and are working sincerely to redress them from within their own areas of expertise. Politicians, civil servants, lawyers, educators, environmentalists, activists, and so on—people from all sides are already engaged in this effort. This is very good so far as it goes, but the fact is, we will never solve our problems simply by instituting new laws and regulations. Ultimately, the source of our problems lies at the level of the individual. If people lack moral values and integrity, no system of laws and regulations will be adequate. So long as people give priority to material values, then injustice, corruption, inequity, intolerance, and greed—all the outward manifestations of neglect of inner values—will persist.

So what are we to do? Where are we to turn for help? Science, for all the benefits it has brought to our external world, has not yet provided scientific grounding for the development of the foundations of personal integrity—the basic inner human values that we appreciate in others and would do well to promote in ourselves. Perhaps then we should seek inner values from religion, as people have done for millennia? Certainly religion has helped millions of people in the past, helps millions today, and will continue to help millions in the future. But for all its benefits in offering moral guidance and meaning in life, in today's secular world religion alone is no longer adequate as a basis for ethics. One reason for this is that many people in the world no longer follow any particular religion. Another reason is that, as the peoples of the world become ever more closely interconnected in an age of globalization and in multicultural societies, ethics based on any one religion would only appeal to some of us; it would not be meaningful for all. In the past, when peoples lived in relative isolation from one another—as we Tibetans lived quite happily for many centuries behind our wall of mountains—the fact that groups pursued their own religiously based approaches to ethics posed no difficulties. Today, however, any religion-based answer to the problem of our neglect of inner values can never be universal, and so will be inadequate. What we need today is an approach to ethics which makes no recourse to religion and can be equally acceptable to those with faith and those without: a secular ethics.

This statement may seem strange coming from someone who from a very early age has lived as a monk in robes. Yet I see no contradiction here. My faith enjoins me to strive for the welfare and benefit of all sentient beings, and reaching out beyond my own tradition, to those of other religions and those of none, is entirely in keeping with this.

I am confident that it is both possible and worthwhile to attempt a new secular approach to universal ethics. My confidence comes from my conviction that all of us, all human beings, are basically inclined or disposed toward what we perceive to be good. Whatever we do, we do because we think it will be of some benefit. At the same time, we all appreciate the kindness of others. We are all, by nature, oriented toward the basic human values of love and compassion. We all prefer the love of others to their hatred. We all prefer others' generosity to their meanness. And who among us does not prefer tolerance, respect, and forgiveness of our failings to bigotry, disrespect, and resentment?

In view of this, I am of the firm opinion that we have within our grasp a way, and a means, to ground inner values without contradicting any religion and yet, crucially, without depending on religion. The development and practice of this new vision of ethics is what I propose to elaborate in the course of this book. It is my hope that doing so will help to promote understanding of the need for ethical awareness and inner values in this age of excessive materialism.

At the outset I should make it clear that my intention is not to dictate moral values. Doing that would be of no benefit. To try to impose moral principles from outside, to impose them, as it were, by command, can never be effective. Instead, I call for each of us to come to our own understanding of the importance of inner values. For it is these inner values which are the source of both an ethically harmonious world and the individual peace of mind, confidence, and happiness we all seek. Of course, all the world's major religions, with their emphasis on love, compassion, patience, tolerance, and forgiveness, can and do promote inner values. But the reality of the world today is that grounding ethics in religion is no longer adequate. This is why I believe the time has come to find a way of thinking about spirituality and ethics that is beyond religion.

Part I

A NEW VISION OF SECULAR ETHICS

1

Rethinking Secularism

Inner Values in an Age of Science

I AM A MAN OF religion, but religion alone cannot answer all our problems.

Not long ago I attended a formal ceremony to mark the opening of a new Buddhist temple in Bihar, a particularly densely populated and poor part of northern India. The chief minister of Bihar, an old friend of mine, made a fine speech in which he expressed his conviction that, with the blessings of the Buddha, the state of Bihar would now prosper. When my turn came to speak, I suggested, half-jokingly, that if Bihar's prosperity depended solely on the blessings of the Buddha, it really should have prospered a long time ago! After all, Bihar is home to the holiest site for Buddhists—Bodh Gaya, where the historical Buddha attained full enlightenment. For real change, we require more than the blessings of the Buddha, powerful though they may be, and more than prayer. We also need action, which will only come about through the able efforts of the chief minister and others like him!

This is not to suggest that blessings and prayer are useless. In fact, I consider prayer to be of immense psychological benefit.

But we must accept that its tangible results are often hard to see. When it comes to obtaining certain, direct results, it is clear that prayer cannot match the achievements of, for instance, modern science. When I was ill some years ago, it was certainly comforting to know that people were praying for me, but it was, I must admit, still more comforting to know that the hospital where I was being treated had the very latest equipment to deal with my condition!

In light of our growing mastery over so many aspects of the physical world in the past two hundred years or so, it is not surprising that many people today question whether we have any need for religion at all. Things which in the past were only dreamt about—the elimination of diseases, space travel, computers—have become reality through science. So it is not surprising that many have come to place all their hopes in science, and even to believe that happiness can be achieved by means of what material science can deliver.

But while I can understand how science has undermined faith in some aspects of traditional religion, I see no reason why advances in science should have the same effect on the notion of inner or spiritual values. Indeed, the need for inner values is more pressing in this age of science than ever before.

In the attempt to make a compelling case for inner values and ethical living in an age of science, it would be ideal to make that case in wholly scientific terms. Although it is not yet possible to do so purely on the basis of scientific research, I am confident that as time goes on, a more and more secure scientific case for the benefits of inner ethical values will gradually emerge.

Of course I am no scientist, and modern science was not a

part of my formal education as a child. However, since coming into exile, I have done a lot of catching up. For more than thirty years now, I have held regular meetings with experts and researchers from many scientific fields, including physics, cosmology, biology, psychology, and, especially of late, neuroscience.

Contemplative traditions, in all religions, place great emphasis on exploring the inner world of experience and consciousness, so one of my aims in these discussions has been to explore the scientific understanding of areas such as thought, emotion, and subjective experience.

I am very encouraged by the fact that science, and particularly neuroscience, is now increasingly paying attention to these matters, which have been neglected for so long. And I am pleased by recent developments in scientific methodology in these areas, in which the traditional scientific principle of objective third-person verifiability is now being expanded to include the domain of subjective experience. An example of this is the work in neurophenomenology by my late friend Francisco Varela.

I have also had a longstanding interest in what scientific basis might be found for understanding the effects of contemplative practice and the deliberate cultivation of qualities such as compassion, loving-kindness, attention, and a calm mind. I have always felt that if science could show such practices to be both possible and beneficial, then perhaps they could even be promoted through mainstream education.

Fortunately, there is now a reasonably substantial body of evidence in evolutionary biology, neuroscience, and other fields suggesting that, even from the most rigorous scientific perspective, unselfishness and concern for others are not only in our own interests but also, in a sense, innate to our biological nature. Such evidence, when combined with reflection on our personal experiences and coupled with simple common sense, can, I believe, offer a strong case for the benefits of cultivating basic human values that does not rely on religious principles or faith at all. And this I welcome.

Approaching Secularism

This then is the basis of what I call "secular ethics." I am aware that for some people, in particular for some Christian and Muslim brothers and sisters, my use of the word "secular" raises difficulties. To some, the very word suggests a firm rejection of, or even hostility toward, religion. It may seem to them that, in using this word, I am advocating the exclusion of religion from ethical systems, or even from all areas of public life. This is not at all what I have in mind. Instead, my understanding of the word "secular" comes from the way it is commonly used in India.

Modern India has a secular constitution and prides itself on being a secular country. In Indian usage, "secular," far from implying antagonism toward religion or toward people of faith, actually implies a profound respect for and tolerance toward all religions. It also implies an inclusive and impartial attitude which includes nonbelievers.

This understanding of the term "secular"—to imply mutual tolerance and respect for all faiths as well as for those of no faith—comes from India's particular historical and cultural background. In the same way, I suspect, the western understanding of the term comes from European history. I am no historian, and certainly no expert on this subject, but it seems to me that as science began to advance rapidly in Europe, there was a move toward greater rationality. And this rationality involved, among other things, a rejection of what came to be seen as the superstitions of the past. For many radical thinkers from that time to our own day, the adoption of rationality has entailed a rejection of religious faith. The French Revolution, which expressed so many of the new ideas of the European Enlightenment, is a good example of this, with its strong anti-religious element. Of course there was also an important social dimension to this rejection. Religion came to be regarded as conservative, tied to tradition, and closely associated with old regimes and all their failings. The legacy of this history, it seems, is that for more than two hundred years, many of the most influential thinkers and reformers in the West have viewed religion, not as an avenue to human liberation, but as an obstacle to progress. Marxism, one of the most powerful secular ideologies of the twentieth century, even denounced religion as the "opium of the people"—with tragic consequences, as communist regimes forcibly suppressed religion in many parts of the world.

It is a result of this history, I feel, that in the West the idea of secularism is so often understood as being antagonistic toward religion. Secularism and religion are often seen as two opposing and mutually incompatible positions, and there is considerable suspicion and hostility between the followers of the two camps.

While I cannot accept the suggestion that religion is an obstacle to human development, I do feel that, in the context of history, anti-religious sentiments may be understandable. History teaches the uncomfortable truth that religious institutions and adherents of every denomination have been involved in exploitation of others at some stage or another. Religion has also been used as a pretext for conflict and oppression. Even Buddhism, with its doctrine of nonviolence, cannot escape this charge entirely.

So when negative attitudes toward religion, in the West or elsewhere, are motivated by a concern for justice, they must be respected. In fact, one could argue that those who point out the hypocrisy of religious people who violate the ethical principles they proclaim, and who stand up against injustices perpetrated by religious figures and institutions, are actually strengthening and benefiting the traditions themselves. However, when assessing such criticisms, it is important to distinguish between criticisms directed at religion itself and those directed at the *institutions* of religion, which are two quite separate things. To my mind, notions of social justice are in no way contrary to the principles espoused by religion itself, because close to the heart of all the great faith traditions is the aim of promoting humanity's most positive qualities and nurturing such values as kindness, compassion, forgiveness, patience, and personal integrity.

Secularism in India

For me, then, the word "secular" holds no fear. Instead, I am mindful of the founders of India's secular constitution, such as Dr. B. R. Ambedkar and Dr. Rajendra Prasad, the latter of whom I had the honor to know personally. Their intention in promoting secularism was not to do away with religion, but rather to recognize formally the religious diversity of Indian society. Mahatma Gandhi, the inspiration behind the constitution, was himself a deeply religious man. In his daily prayer meetings, he included readings and hymns from all the country's major faith traditions. This remarkable example is followed in Indian public ceremonies to this day.

The kind of religious tolerance Gandhi personified is nothing new in India. It has ancient roots, stretching back more than two thousand years. It is revealed, for example, on inscribed pillars dating from the reign of Emperor Ashoka in the third century BCE. One inscription contains the exhortation to "honor another's religion, for doing so strengthens both one's own and that of the other." Furthermore, Sanskrit literature reveals a classical culture that was intellectually tolerant and rich in debate. In India, many philosophical positions have been subjects of great discussion since ancient times. Even positions that look much like modern materialism and atheism have an honorable and respected history in Indian tradition. Classical philosophical texts contain many references to the Charvaka school, whose adherents rejected any idea of God and the existence of any soul or afterlife. Other thinkers often vigorously opposed Charvaka views as nihilistic, but their radical materialism was nevertheless taken seriously as a philosophical position, and their founder was generally referred to as a *rishi* (sage). Proponents of Charvaka ideas were also accorded a certain level of recognition and respect by some Indian rulers—many of whom were outstandingly tolerant of other religious faiths. The Muslim Emperor Akbar, who held dialogues with Hindus, Christians, and others, is one example of this tradition.

Some time ago, I had an illuminating discussion on this subject with a former deputy prime minister of India, Mr. L. K. Advani. He suggested that India's longstanding culture of tolerance, diversity, and debate is precisely what explains its marked success in maintaining a secular democracy. I am sure he is right. Today, the majority in India are Hindu, but many other religions are also well represented. India is home to the second-largest Muslim population in the world—a fact not appreciated by many in the West—and there are also many millions of Sikhs and Christians, as well as substantial Jain, Buddhist, Zoroastrian, and Jewish communities. In fact, the ethnic and religious minorities of India are almost too numerous to mention. In addition, hundreds of different languages are spoken in the country today. Amid this tremendous human diversity, it is a relatively common sight to see Hindu temples and Muslim minarets standing next to one another on city streets. In fact, most villages have more than one religion represented among their populations.

I recently met a man from Romania who, for a research project, had visited numerous Indian villages. In telling me about a largely Muslim village in Rajasthan in which there were only three Hindu families, he expressed surprise that these families lived there with no sense of fear or apprehension. His surprise, I thought, must be a result of the western media's misleading portrayal of India's communal relations. There have been some severe and deeply regrettable incidents of communal violence in India, but it is a mistake to generalize these across the entire subcontinent. Notwithstanding such isolated incidents,

India by and large maintains, despite its great diversity, a peaceful and harmonious society. Clearly, the ancient Indian doctrine of *ahimsa,* or nonviolence, has flourished and been adopted as a principle of peaceful coexistence by all faiths. This is a tremendous achievement, and one from which other countries in the world can learn.

Tolerance in an Age of Globalization

Sometimes I describe myself as a modern-day messenger of ancient Indian thought. Two of the most important ideas I share wherever I travel—the principles of nonviolence and interreligious harmony—are both drawn from ancient Indian heritage. Though I am of course a Tibetan, I also consider myself to be, in a sense, a son of India. Since childhood my mind has been nourished by the classics of Indian thought. From the age of six, when I began my studies as a monk, the majority of the texts I read and memorized were by Indian Buddhist masters, many of whom were from the ancient university of Nalanda in central India. And since early adulthood my body, too, has been nourished by Indian fare: rice and *dal* (lentils).

So I am very happy to share and promote this Indian understanding of secularism, as I believe it can be of great value to all humanity. In today's interconnected and globalized world, it is now commonplace for people of dissimilar world views, faiths, and races to live side by side. I am often struck by this on my travels, especially in the West. For a considerable portion of humanity today, it is possible and indeed likely that one's neighbor, one's colleague, or one's employer will have a different mother tongue, eat different food, and follow a different religion than oneself.

It is a matter of great urgency, therefore, that we find ways to cooperate with one another in a spirit of mutual acceptance and respect. For while to many people it is a source of joy to live in a cosmopolitan environment where they can experience a wide spectrum of different cultures, there is no doubt that, for others, living in close proximity with those who do not share their language or culture can pose difficulties. It can create confusion, fear, and resentment, leading in the worst cases to open hostility and new ideologies of exclusion based on race, nationality, or religion. Unfortunately, as we look around the world, we see that social tensions are actually quite common. Furthermore, it seems likely that, as economic migration continues, such difficulties may even increase.

In such a world, I feel, it is vital for us to find a genuinely sustainable and universal approach to ethics, inner values, and personal integrity—an approach that can transcend religious, cultural, and racial differences and appeal to people at a fundamental human level. This search for a sustainable, universal approach is what I call the project of secular ethics.

As I go on to elaborate this approach, I should acknowledge that there are some who, though sympathetic to my explanation of secularism in Indian terms, still question the viability of detaching ethics from religion in this way. The mistrust of attempts to separate the two is so strong among some followers of theistic traditions that I have been cautioned, on some occasions, not to use the word "secular" when speaking about ethics in public.

Clearly there are people who believe, with complete sincerity, that separating ethics from religion is a great mistake in itself, and indeed is a source of many of the social and moral problems of modern society—the breakdown of families, growing numbers of abortions, sexual promiscuity, alcoholism, drug addiction, and so on. For them, these problems largely result from people having lost the basis for developing inner values that religion alone can provide. For those whose religious belief is so closely tied to ethical practice, it is hard to conceive of one without the other. For those who believe that truth requires God, God alone can make ethics binding. Without God as the guarantor, they suggest, there is at best only relative truth, so that what is true for one person may not be true for another. And in this situation there is no basis for distinguishing right from wrong, for evaluating good and bad, or for restraining selfish and destructive impulses and cultivating inner values.

While I fully respect this point of view, it is not one I share. I do not agree that ethics requires grounding in religious concepts or faith. Instead, I firmly believe that ethics can also emerge simply as a natural and rational response to our very humanity and our common human condition.

Religion and Ethics

Though this book is not primarily about religion, in the interest of mutual understanding and respect between those with faith and those without it, I think it is worth spending a little time considering the relationship between religion and ethics.

For thousands of years, religion has been at the heart of human civilization. It is little wonder, then, that a concern for others and the basic inner values that emerge from this concern, such as kindness, honesty, patience, and forgiveness, have long been largely formulated in religious terms. In all of the world's major faith traditions, both theistic and non-theistic, these values, as well as those of self-discipline, contentment, and generosity, are celebrated as the keys to living a meaningful and worthwhile life. There is no surprise in this. Since religion's primary concern is with the human spirit, it is entirely natural that the practice of these inner values—which brings such rewards in terms of our own spiritual well-being and that of those around us—should be integral to any religious practice.

The systems of belief with which the world's religions ground and support inner values can, generally speaking, be grouped into two categories.

On the one hand are the theistic religions, which include Hinduism, Sikhism, Zoroastrianism, Judaism, Christianity, and Islam. In these traditions, ethics is ultimately grounded in some understanding of God—as a creator and as the absolute ground of all that is. From a theistic point of view, the entire universe is part of a divine creation and plan, so the very fabric of that universe is sacred. And since God is infinite love or infinite compassion, loving others is part of loving and serving God. Also in many theistic traditions there is the belief that after death we will face divine judgment, and this provides a further strong incentive for behaving with restraint and due caution while here on Earth. When undertaken seriously, submission to God can have a powerful effect in reducing self-centeredness, and can thereby lay the foundation for a very secure ethical and even altruistic outlook.

On the other hand, in the non-theistic religions, such as Buddhism, Jainism, and a branch of the ancient Indian Samkhya school, there is no belief in a divine creator. Instead, there is the core principle of causality, while the universe is regarded as beginningless. Without a creator figure in which to ground inner values and an ethical life, the non-theistic religions instead ground ethics in the idea of karma. The Sanskrit word *karma* simply means "action." So when we talk about our karma, we are referring to all our intentional acts of body, speech, and mind, and when we talk about the *fruits* of our karma, we are talking about the consequences of these acts. The doctrine of karma is grounded in the observation of causality as a law of nature. Every intended action, word, or thought we have has a potentially unending stream of consequences. When combined with the idea of rebirth and successive lives, this understanding becomes a powerful basis for ethics and the cultivation of inner values. For example, a key Buddhist teaching on the cultivation of compassion involves, as part of establishing deep empathetic connection with all beings, viewing all beings as having been one's mother at some stage in one's countless previous lives.

All religions, therefore, to some extent, ground the cultivation of inner values and ethical awareness in some kind of metaphysical (that is, not empirically demonstrable) understanding of the world and of life after death. And just as the doctrine of divine judgment underlies ethical teachings in many theistic religions, so too does the doctrine of karma and future lives in non-theistic religions.

In the context of religion, these understandings—whether theistic or non-theistic—are of immense importance, since they provide the foundations not only for the determination to live ethically, but also for salvation or liberation itself. As such, for religious practitioners, the pursuit of an ethical life and their ultimate spiritual aspirations are inseparable.

I am not among those who think that humans will soon be ready to dispense with religion altogether. On the contrary, in my view, faith is a force for good and can be tremendously beneficial. In offering an understanding of human life which transcends our temporary physical existence, religion gives hope and strength to those facing adversity. The value of the world's great faith traditions is a subject I have discussed at some length in a previous book, *Toward a True Kinship of Faiths*. For all its benefits, however—in bringing people together, giving guidance and solace, and offering a vision of the good life which people can strive to emulate—I do not think that religion is indispensable to the spiritual life.

But where does this leave us with regard to grounding ethics and nurturing inner values? Today, in a scientific age in which religion strikes many as meaningless, what basis for such values is left to us? How can we find a way of motivating ourselves ethically without recourse to traditional beliefs?

To my mind, although humans can manage without religion, they cannot manage without inner values. So my argument for the independence of ethics from religion is quite simple. As I see it, spirituality has two dimensions. The first dimension, that of basic spiritual well-being—by which I mean inner mental and emotional strength and balance—does not depend on religion but comes from our innate human nature as beings with a natural disposition toward compassion, kindness, and caring for others. The second dimension is what may be considered religion-based spirituality, which is acquired from our upbringing and culture and is tied to particular beliefs and practices. The difference between the two is something like the difference between water and tea. Ethics and inner values without religious content are like water, something we *need* every day for health and survival. Ethics and inner values based in a religious context are more like tea. The tea we drink is mostly composed of water, but it also contains some other ingredients—tea leaves, spices, perhaps some sugar or, at least in Tibet, salt—and this makes it more nutritious and sustaining and something we want every day. But however the tea is prepared, the primary ingredient is always water. While we can live without tea, we can't live without water. Likewise we are born free of religion, but we are not born free of the need for compassion.

More fundamental than religion, therefore, is our basic human spirituality. We have an underlying human disposition toward love, kindness, and affection, irrespective of whether we have a religious framework or not. When we nurture this most fundamental human resource—when we set about cultivating those inner values which we all appreciate in others—then we start to live spiritually. The challenge, therefore, is to find a way of grounding ethics and supporting the cultivation of inner values that is in keeping with the scientific age, while not neglecting the deeper needs of the human spirit, which, for many people, religion answers.

Grounding Ethics in Human Nature

Across all cultures, all philosophies, and indeed all individual perspectives, there is no consensus about the essential orientation of human nature. Instead, there seem to be many views. To put the matter at its simplest, there are some who believe, at one end of the spectrum, that we are by nature fundamentally violent, aggressive, and competitive; while others, at the other end, take the view that we are predominantly disposed toward gentleness and love. Most perspectives lie between these extremes, accommodating all of our qualities and propensities in varying degrees. Generally speaking, if we view human nature as dominated by destructive tendencies, our ethics will most likely be grounded in something outside ourselves. We will understand ethics as a means for keeping those destructive tendencies in check in the name of some greater good. If, however, we view human nature as predominantly oriented toward kindness and the desire for a peaceful life, then we can consider ethics an entirely natural and rational means for pursuing our innate potential. On this understanding, ethics consists less of rules to be obeyed than of principles for inner self-regulation to promote those aspects of our nature which we recognize as conducive to our own well-being and that of others. This second approach is in tune with my own.

Two Pillars for Secular Ethics

I believe that an inclusive approach to secular ethics, one with the potential to be universally accepted, requires recognition of only two basic principles. Both of these can easily be grasped on the basis of our common experience as humans and our common sense, and both are supported by findings of contemporary research, particularly in fields such as psychology, neuroscience, and the clinical sciences. The first principle is the recognition of our *shared humanity* and our shared aspiration to happiness and the avoidance of suffering; the second is the understanding of *interdependence* as a key feature of human reality, including our biological reality as social animals. From these two principles we can learn to appreciate the inextricable connection between our own well-being and that of others, and we can develop a genuine concern for others' welfare. Together, I believe, they constitute an adequate basis for establishing ethical awareness and the cultivation of inner values. It is through such values that we gain a sense of connection with others, and it is by moving beyond narrow self-interest that we find meaning, purpose, and satisfaction in life.

Before offering a systematic presentation of the way I envisage this secular approach, a few words are in order on the background and motivation that shape my views on this subject.

Since childhood I have been a Buddhist monk in the Tibetan Mahayana tradition. My understanding of ethics, as well as of issues such as human nature and the pursuit of happiness, is informed by this background. On a personal level, my everyday approach to the practice of ethics is profoundly influenced by the writings of the Indian Nalanda tradition, which combines critical philosophical inquiry with ethical living and contemplative practice. In the course of this book I draw on some of the resources of the Nalanda tradition. However, it is certainly not my intention, in presenting this book, to make more Buddhists! In fact, when I am asked to give Buddhist teachings in the West, I often share my personal view that it is not, by and large, a good idea for people to adopt religious practices which are not well grounded in their own culture and educational background. To do so can be difficult and can lead to unnecessary confusion. Instead, my motivation is simply a wish to contribute to the betterment of humanity. If resources from my own tradition can be useful to those outside it, then I think it is good to draw on those resources. In writing this book I am certainly not interested in propagating my own faith. Instead, I am calling on my readers to investigate matters for themselves. If they find some of the insights of classical Indian thought useful in their investigations, that is excellent, but if not, that is also okay!

So, in the following chapters, I offer my thoughts not as a Buddhist, nor as a religious believer, but simply as one human being among nearly seven billion others, one who cares about the fate of humanity and wants to do something to safeguard and improve its future.

2

Our Common Humanity

How We See Ourselves

As a matter of observation, how people treat their fellow human beings, and indeed the world around them, largely depends on how they conceive of themselves. We all have many different ways of seeing "who we are," and these different views influence our behavior. For instance, we may consider ourselves in terms of gender as men or women, or as followers of this or that religion, or as members of this or that race or nationality. We may think of ourselves in terms of family—as a father or a mother, for instance. We may also identify with our occupation, our level of education, or our achievements. Depending on which perspective we take, we raise different expectations of ourselves. And this in turn affects our behavior, including our treatment of other people.

Everyone has his or her own separate identity. Because of this, it is of primary importance, in any attempt to develop a genuinely universal approach to ethics, to have a clear understanding of what unites us all, namely our common humanity. We are all human, all seven billion of us. In this respect we are all one hundred percent the same.

To begin then, let us consider what it is that actually makes us human. Well, first of all, it is our simple physical reality: this body of ours, made up of so many parts, bones, muscles, blood—so many molecules, atoms, and so on.

At the basic material level, there is no qualitative difference between the matter that makes up a human being and, for example, the matter that makes up a lump of rock. In terms of material constitution, a lump of rock and our human bodies are both ultimately made up of aggregations of minute particles. Modern science suggests that all the matter of the cosmos is being endlessly recycled. Many scientists even hold the view that the very atoms in our bodies once belonged to stars far away in time and space.

Yet it is clearly the case that a human being belongs to quite a different category of things from a lump of rock. We are born, we grow, and then we die, as do plants and all other animals. However, unlike plants, we also have conscious experience. We feel pain, and we experience pleasure. We are sentient beings, what in Tibetan we call *semden.*

During one of my many discussions with my late friend the neurobiologist Francisco Varela, we talked about what it is that distinguishes sentient forms of life from plant forms of life. As I recall, he suggested as a criterion "an entity's ability to move itself from here to there," or words to that effect. If an organism can move its whole body from one place to another to escape danger and survive, or to obtain food and to reproduce, then it may be regarded as a sentient being. This definition interested me, since it implies that, even from a scientific point of view, what defines such a living being has something to do with the ability to feel pleasure and pain, and to respond to these feelings, even if the responses are predominantly or even entirely instinctive. At the most basic level, the ability to respond to one's surroundings with conscious experience is what we can consider, in the broadest sense, "mind."

This is not the place to embark on a lengthy treatment of the vast issue of what constitutes "mind" and the ways in which the human mind is distinguished from that of other beings, so a few words will have to suffice here.

The primary ingredients of human experience, according to modern science, are the data of our senses—sight, sound, touch, taste, and smell. At another level of perception are our subjective experiences of these basic sensations: whether we experience them as being pleasant, unpleasant, neutral, or some combination of these. As far as we know, we share this kind of apprehension of sensory experience as pleasurable or painful with other animals. Birds and mammals, for example, seem to apprehend sensory experience in a manner very similar to ours, while other types of animals, such as fish or insects, seem to differ from us considerably in this respect.

However wide and varied the spectrum of sentience may be across different kinds of animals, it is apparent that all beings which have conscious experience are oriented toward the pursuit of those experiences which are pleasant and the avoidance of those which are unpleasant or painful. In this fundamental respect, we humans are no different from other animals. Like them, we seek to avoid suffering and are naturally drawn toward experiences that are pleasant or happy.

But if this fundamental orientation is a defining feature of sentient beings in general, humans constitute a rather special category. Clearly there is more to being human than merely responding to sensory experience. We are not like dogs or cats, for instance, which, by and large, respond to their experiences purely on instinct. We humans have evolved, over many thousands of years, a tremendous complexity, which distinguishes us from all other animals. This difference is reflected in the large size of our brains, which have a much more developed frontal cortex than the brains of other species.

Human Consciousness and Empathy

In discussing the complexity of the human mind, I am not just thinking of our intellectual or rational processes and our ability for self-reflection, but rather of the entire range of our conscious experience, which includes not just thoughts, imagination, and memory but also feelings and emotions. In fact, when I talk about "mind" or "experience" in this rather general way, I am usually thinking of the Tibetan words *sem* (mind) and *shepa* (cognition), both of which refer not just to the predominantly intellectual activities normally associated with words such as "mind" and "mental" in English and other western languages, but rather to all areas of our inner experience, including feelings and emotions which in those languages are often described as matters of the *heart.*

Some time ago, western scientists began to conduct neuroscientific tests on long-term Tibetan meditators, to measure the biological effects of their contemplative practices. On one occasion, I was told, the scientists were giving a talk on their experiment to a group of monks at the Namgyal monastery here in Dharamsala. To demonstrate their techniques, one of the scientists wore on his head a white cap from which protruded a great mass of wires and electrodes. On seeing him, some of the monks burst out laughing. The scientists assumed they were laughing at the strange sight of a western scientist with wires attached to his head. But it turned out they were also laughing in surprise that the wires were only attached to the head and not to any other areas of the body. After all, if the intention was to measure qualities such as compassion or loving-kindness, wouldn't other parts of the body, such as the heart, be equally important? These days, we are better versed in the contemporary scientific models and are no longer so surprised by the centrality that modern science accords to the brain. And the scientists too have changed their methods somewhat: they now include measurements to detect changes in the heart.

As to what distinguishes the human mind from the minds of other beings, a few major features are immediately apparent. We humans have a strong and subtle capacity for remembering, seemingly much greater than those of many other animals, which allows us to project our thoughts into the past. We also have the ability to project our thoughts into the future. In addition, we have very powerful imaginations and a highly developed capacity for communication through symbolic language. And, perhaps most distinctively, we have the capacity for rational thought—the ability to critically evaluate and compare different outcomes in both real and imaginary situations. While other animals may possess some of these capacities to a limited degree, they do not match humans in their level of sophistication.

Along with these characteristics, we have a further quality which is central to our identity as human beings: our instinctive capacity for empathy. Of course we are not alone in this. Some other animals exhibit behavior that seems to indicate empathy. Nonetheless, it is an essential human trait. When we see someone in pain, even a stranger on the street or a victim of natural disaster we see on television or hear about on the radio, we have an instinctive response to his or her suffering. And not only that, we also experience an instinctive urge, whether we act upon it or not, to do something about it—to help that stranger on the street, or to ease the sufferings of those we see on television.

In the same way, when we witness people triumphing over adversity, our instinctive ability to empathize with the experiences of others allows us to share their joy. I think part of the reason so many of us love to watch films, sports, and plays, to read entertaining books, and so on, is that, in addition to the thrills they bring, they give us the chance to feel others' joys and sorrows as if they were our own. We naturally enjoy empathetic experience and often seek it out in our lives. An example is the joy we take in the delight of small children—we love to see their faces light up when we smile at them, give them something, or tell them a story. In the same way, we naturally enjoy the happiness of our loved ones. Everyone prefers to see others smiling rather than frowning.

Since we are social animals—that is, since our survival and

flourishing depend on being part of a group or community —our capacity for empathy has profound implications for our pursuit of happiness and well-being.

Happiness and Suffering

That we all seek a happy life is, I think, a claim which needs no justification. No one wishes for difficulties or troubles. This is something that the very constitution of our bodies confirms. Medical science increasingly suggests that a person who is happy and peaceful, free from fear and anxiety, will enjoy tangible health benefits. It is also a matter of common sense that even people afflicted by illness are much better off if they have a positive outlook. So I consider it a simple truth that this body of ours is meant for a happy life. A happy mind is a healthy mind, and a healthy mind is good for the body.

But human happiness and suffering, unlike those of other animals, are not straightforward. A dog may find happiness by eating a good meal and then going onto the veranda to lie down. While we may relate to such simple pleasures, it is clear that they are in no way sufficient for genuine human satisfaction.

The never-ending human quest for happiness and avoidance of suffering explains not only humankind's greatest achievements but also the evolution, over many millennia, of this large brain of ours. Even the very concept of religion, I think, has arisen from this quest. For in the course of life we inevitably face problems that are beyond our ability to control. To maintain hope and to keep our spirits up, therefore, we develop faith, and to support faith we turn to prayer, and prayer is a core element of religion. Similarly, I would suggest, the extraordinary human achievements in science and technological innovation over the past few centuries also stem from the urge to overcome suffering and achieve happiness.

However, although our extraordinary mental sophistication distinguishes us humans from other forms of life and drives our astonishing success as a species, this very mental complexity is, at the same time, the source of many of our most enduring difficulties and hardships. Most of the problems we face in the world today—such as armed conflict, poverty, injustice, and environmental degradation—have arisen and are maintained by complex human activity. Furthermore, our most persistent sources of inner suffering at an individual level—fear, anxiety, and stress, for example—are also closely connected to our mental complexity and our excitable imaginations.

Fundamental Equality

In our quest for happiness and the avoidance of suffering, we are all fundamentally the same, and therefore equal. This is an important point. For if we can integrate an appreciation of this fundamental human equality into our everyday outlook, I am very confident that it will be of immense benefit, not only to society at large, but also to us as individuals. For myself, whenever I meet people—whether they are presidents or beggars, whether dark or fair, short or tall, rich or poor, from this nation or that, of this faith or that—I try to relate to them simply as human beings who, like me, seek happiness and wish to avoid suffering. Adopting this perspective, I find, generates a natural feeling of closeness even with those who until that moment were complete strangers to me. Despite all our individual characteristics, no matter what education we may have or what social rank we may have inherited, and irrespective of what we may have achieved in our lives, we all seek to find happiness and to avoid suffering during this short life of ours.

For this reason, I often make the point that the factors which divide us are actually much more superficial than those we share. Despite all the characteristics that differentiate us—race, language, religion, gender, wealth, and many others—we are all equal in terms of our basic humanity. And this equality is corroborated by science. The sequencing of the human genome, for example, has shown that racial differences constitute only a tiny fraction of our genetic makeup, the vast majority of which is shared by all of us. In fact, at the genome level, the differences between individuals appear more pronounced than those between different races.

In light of these considerations, the time has come, I believe, for each one of us to start thinking and acting on the basis of an identity rooted in the phrase "*we* human beings."

3

The Quest for Happiness

A HUMAN BEING survives only with hope, and hope by definition implies the thought of something better. As I see it, our very survival depends on some idea of future happiness. But if we accept that human beings are fundamentally oriented toward the pursuit of happiness and the avoidance of suffering, it remains to be explored what is meant by happiness, and where it might come from. Happiness is a rather general term, so there is potential for misunderstanding. For example, it should be made clear that in this book's secular context, we are not talking about religious conceptions of ultimate happiness, but rather the simple joy or happiness we all understand in an ordinary or everyday sense.

As I noted earlier, for beings of our complexity, achieving happiness is not straightforward. Unlike dog or cat happiness, for example, human happiness requires more than the simple satisfaction of sensory appetite. So what are the sources of human happiness?

Three factors immediately suggest themselves which, I think most people will agree, contribute significantly to human well-being, namely wealth or prosperity; health; and friendship or companionship.

Wealth, Health, and Friendship

Let us start with wealth. Does our material situation affect our happiness? Well, certainly it does! It would be foolish to deny the importance of material factors to our well-being. After all, even a hermit living alone in a mountain cave needs food and clothing. Without a certain level of material comfort, people cannot live with the dignity we all deserve as humans. Of course money is an important factor in our quest to avoid suffering and achieve happiness.

But how much money is enough? In Tibetan we sometimes call money by the nickname Kunga Dhondup. To Tibetan ears, this sounds like an ordinary personal name, but it means something like "that which makes us all happy and can fulfill our wishes." Since money gives us choices and freedom, it is natural that people find it very alluring and can't seem to get enough of it. Occasionally I tease my Tibetan audiences about their devotion to Kunga Dhondup. You see, as part of our traditional religious practice, we Tibetans generally recite a mantra associated with the Buddha of Compassion, "*Om mani padme hum.*" We do this frequently throughout the day, often under our breath, even when we are busy with other things: "Om mani padme hum," we say, "om mani padme hum." But when people recite it quickly, it gets a bit mumbled—"om mani padme, om mani padme . . . mani padme . . . Om mani . . . mani . . . mani"—at which point it starts to sound as if they are speaking English, and saying "money, money, money"!

But again, and joking aside, of course wealth and prosperity bring benefits. As humans we need decent shelter, a healthy environment, nutritious food, and clean water. These are our fundamental needs—and as such are prerequisites of human happiness.

However, while the further benefits of wealth—a new house, a new car, a new telephone perhaps—may provide some temporary increase in our level of comfort or daily convenience, there is no guarantee that they will bring any lasting satisfaction or contribute to an overall sense of well-being. In fact, acquiring ever more possessions often leads to greater anxiety, stress, and worry. And these factors can in turn feed anger and even resentment.

Interestingly, evidence compiled by psychologists and social scientists in recent years suggests quite clearly that material acquisitions have only temporary effects on what they call "mental flourishing." Such studies suggest that after the initial excitement of a new purchase has worn off, our level of happiness quickly returns to its previous level. In spoken Tibetan we have an expression which captures this phenomenon quite well, and I do not know of an exact equivalent in other languages. When a person is particularly drawn to the thrill of new acquisitions, we call that person *asar tsapo,* "very *asar,*" where *sar* means "new." The implication is that such a person is not just greedy but excitable and fickle—always running after the latest trend or the newest gadget. I think modern consumerist culture tends to encourage this kind of fickleness.

From conflict over resources in the natural world to conflict within families, material values are so often a source of trouble. And material wealth is no guarantor of happiness. In fact I have met quite a few very rich people, billionaires even, who confide that personally they are quite dissatisfied and unhappy with their lives. Wealth creates a kind of cocoon around people which often brings loneliness. So Kunga Dhondup is an unreliable friend who also brings a lot of suffering. While material wealth can be a source of so much stress and unhappiness, mental wealth, based on love and compassion, cannot. It is obvious, therefore, which kind of wealth we should really seek.

But, you might say, wealth confers a kind of security and satisfaction that is in fact quite lasting. Perhaps this is true, but how secure, really, can material wealth ever be? Periodic natural disasters remind us of how fragile the material security we feel actually is.

Much more important than money, possessions, or status, therefore, is our inner or mental state of being. Members of a poor family will be happy if there is affection, kindness, and trust between them. Their rich neighbors may live in luxury, but if suspicion or resentment besets their minds, they will have no genuine happiness. This is a matter of common sense. So ultimately the mental level is key.

Recent social science research has shown not only that the mental benefits of wealth are temporary, but also that the general level of contentment in a society is higher when wealth is more evenly distributed among the population than when there are large disparities between rich and poor. This again suggests that well-being cannot be measured in objective material terms, but is dependent on a range of contextual factors which affect one's mental attitude toward or relationship to that wealth.

And what about health? Is health a source of well-being? Once again, it certainly is. As most of us have experienced for ourselves, when we are in constant pain or discomfort, maintaining a positive attitude can be very difficult. So, looking after our physical health is crucial. We must eat well, sleep well, and take some exercise. If we fall ill, we should consult a suitably qualified doctor and follow the treatment prescribed. This much is obvious. If, however, we consider health to be an entirely physical matter, and concern ourselves only with the state of our body while neglecting mental and emotional factors, then we are mistaken. For there is no necessary or direct link between enjoying good physical health and being happy. After all, isn't it possible for someone with a healthy, strong body to be unhappy? In fact it is quite common. And isn't it equally possible for someone in poor, even very poor health nonetheless to be happy? I am sure it is. Does the physical frailty of, say, very old people necessarily entail unhappiness? Certainly not! So, although physical health certainly contributes to human happiness, it is not its ultimate source. Instead, the real source of happiness once again involves our state of mind, outlook, and motivation, and our level of warmheartedness toward others.

Now let us consider friendship. Certainly, having a close circle of friends, people with whom we can pass time and share experiences, is very important. As we are social animals, relationships with others are crucial to our well-being. But we must consider carefully what distinguishes genuine friendship from superficial relationships, which bring only superficial benefits. There is no doubt that, in human society, money, social standing, and appearance bring with them a great deal of attention. Yet what is the real object of this attention? Is it possible that these people are not truly our friends but rather friends of our money, status, or good looks? And if so, what will happen if our fortunes decline? What if we lose our good looks or our money? Will these friends still be there when we need them, or will they just fade away? The danger is that such friends will quickly disappear.

It is clearly the case that genuine friendship can only be based on trust and affection, which can only arise when there is a mutual sense of concern and respect. So feelings of trust and loving-kindness, which counteract feelings of isolation or loneliness, do not come from the mere external presence of others, or from the outer appearance of friendship, but from one's own attitude of concern and respect toward those others. Their ultimate source is within us.

During a visit to Spain many years ago, I met a Christian monk who had spent five years living as a hermit behind his monastery. I asked him what he had been doing all that time. He replied that he had been meditating on love. When he said this, in English even more broken than mine, I saw such a depth of feeling in his eyes that there was no need for him to say more. Here we have an example of someone who lived alone but felt no loneliness. It is warmheartedness or compassion, above all, which connects us to others. People who appear to have many friends and admirers may nevertheless feel quite isolated. I would remind such people that the only antidote to such loneliness is their own inner attitude of affection, concern, and warm-heartedness toward their fellow human beings.

Two Levels of Satisfaction

These considerations reveal that when we speak about happiness we are often mixing up two quite different and largely independent states—two levels of satisfaction. On the one hand, there are those pleasurable feelings which come with sensory-level experiences. Wealth, health, and friendship all contribute greatly to such feelings. On the other hand, there is a deeper level of satisfaction, deriving not from external stimuli but from our own mental state. It is this second level of satisfaction, coming from within us, which I refer to when I talk about genuine human happiness.

The first kind of satisfaction, since it is dependent on sensory stimulation, is by its nature fragile and transient. Such pleasures last only so long as the sensory stimulation, and when this is over, they make no lasting contribution to our overall sense of well-being. For example, many people spend a great deal of time watching sporting events. But after the event, what is left? What long-term benefit has been gained?

All pleasures based on sensory stimulation derive at some level from the satisfaction of a craving. And if we become obsessed with satisfying that craving, this will eventually turn into a kind of suffering. Even the pleasure we get from eating turns to suffering if we overindulge.

I do not want to suggest that such pleasures are completely worthless, but simply to point out that the satisfactions they bring are transient and involve self-perpetuating cycles of craving. In today's materialistic world, in which inner values are often neglected, it is very easy to fall into the habit of constantly seeking sensory stimulation. Often I notice that if people are not listening to music, watching television, talking on the telephone, and so on, they feel bored or restless and don't know what to do. This suggests that their sense of well-being is heavily dependent on the sensory level of satisfaction.

What about the other, inner level of satisfaction? Where does it come from? And how can it be achieved? Well, first of all, genuine happiness requires peace of mind or a degree of mental composure. When this is present, hardship counts for little. With the strength and mental stability derived from inner peace, we can endure all kinds of adversity.

The role of our minds in determining our happiness can be easily illustrated. Imagine two people diagnosed with the same terminal illness, say an advanced form of untreatable cancer. One of them responds to this news with anger and self-pity, obsessively focusing on the unfairness of the situation, while the other responds with calm acceptance. In both cases the material condition, in terms of physical health and suffering, is the same. But the first person incurs additional psychological and emotional pain, while the person with a calm mind is better equipped to carry on with life and continue to experience the things that bring joy—family perhaps, or dedication to certain causes, or reading. The only difference between the two is in their state of mind.

With inner resilience it is possible, even in extremely aggravating circumstances, to maintain a degree of happiness. And yet, without this inner strength, no amount of sensual gratification can ever make us happy.

But if peace of mind is our first defense against hardship and suffering, there are also other crucial factors which greatly contribute to our level of genuine happiness and joy. Recent scientific research suggests that chief among these are a sense of purpose which transcends narrow self-interest and a feeling of being connected with others or of belonging to a community. The root of both of these, I believe, is compassion or warmheartedness, and it is to this that I now turn.

4

Compassion, the Foundation of Well-Being

LIKE ALL OTHER mammals, we humans are born from our mothers, and for some time after birth we are utterly dependent on attention of our mothers or other caring adults. For nine months we are nurtured in our mother's womb, and at the moment of birth we are completely helpless. We can neither sit nor crawl, let alone stand or walk, and without the care and attention of others we cannot survive. In this state of absolute vulnerability, our first act as a newborn baby is to suck at our mother's breast. And with her milk we are nurtured and given strength. In fact the period of dependency for young humans is particularly long. This goes for all of us, including even the worst criminals. Without another's loving care, none of us would have lived more than a few days. As a result of this intense need for others in our early development, a disposition toward affection is a part of our biology.

This is a characteristic we share with many other mammals, and also birds—all those creatures whose early survival depends on receiving care from others. All such animals clearly experience some kind of feeling of connection or bonding. Even if we can't quite call it affection, they all have some kind of feeling of closeness. In contrast, we are unlike turtles or butterflies, which lay their eggs and then leave them, never to see their offspring again. For such animals there is no period of nurture, so I wonder if they can appreciate affection. Recently, during a talk at Oxford University, I suggested, only half joking, that the scientists in the audience might do some research into this. Do those animals that do not require any period of nurture recognize their parents, for example? Somehow I doubt it. It is something I would be very interested to observe.

But for humans, with our prolonged period of nurture, the role of others' concern and affection is obviously crucial to our survival and well-being. Recent medical research shows that the very physical touch of one's mother or caregiver during early infancy is a crucial factor in the physical enlargement of the brain. And modern psychology confirms that the care we receive as infants and children has a profound impact on our emotional and psychological development. This research also shows that people who lack affection as children are more likely to have a deep-seated sense of insecurity in later life.

A program that I came to know some years ago is working to improve the care provided by orphanages in some troubled parts of Latin America. The measures this program promotes are the fruit of considerable scientific and psychological research, but they are also quite simple, really matters of common sense, since they all reflect the crucial role of human warmth and affection in our mental and physical development. The measures include, for example, housing children in smaller, more intimate dormitories, and assigning them in small groups to individual caregivers so they have a chance to develop something like natural family relationships. In the case of babies, caregivers are encouraged to use plenty of physical contact and to talk to the children and look into their eyes when changing their nappies and so on. Such measures, though simple, can have an impact which lasts a lifetime.

Our dependence on others is most apparent in childhood, but it does not end there. Whenever we face difficulties in life, we turn to others for support. When we are ill, for instance, we go to a doctor. Throughout our lives, even our physical health benefits from simple human affection and warmth. Recovery itself is not just a matter of receiving the right medical treatment or putting the right chemicals into our bloodstream, but is also dependent to a significant degree on the human care we receive.

This point was reinforced for me recently when I underwent an operation in Delhi to remove my gallbladder. It was meant to be a minor operation, but there were some complications, and what should have been a twenty-minute procedure took four hours, and I had to spend a few days recovering in the hospital. Fortunately, the doctors and nurses there were very kind and warmhearted toward me, and I remember a great deal of joy and laughter. I have little doubt that my speedy recovery was considerably helped by the environment of human warmth and happiness they helped create.

We also depend greatly on the warmth and kindness of others when we reach the end of our lives. How much better it is to depart from this world surrounded by love and affection, in an environment of peace and happiness, than to be surrounded by indifference or hostility, in an environment of discord and resentment. Considered from a purely rational point of view, the way others feel about us when we are about to die should not matter to us, since when we are gone, their attitudes cannot affect us. But in fact we care intensely. At the point of death, the goodwill of others matters to us profoundly. This is simply a fact of human nature.

Of course, humans are not alone in this dependence on the warmth and affection of others. Scientific studies yield similar conclusions with regard to various other mammals that also require nurture. For example, I recently heard a presentation by some scientists concerning the behavior of monkeys. They had observed that young monkeys who lived with their mothers were, by and large, more playful and less quarrelsome than those separated from their mothers at birth. The ones that had been separated from their mothers exhibited aggressive behavior, suggesting that they were emotionally agitated and lacking an inner sense of security. Another study demonstrated the role of grooming in the early physical development of rats. Even rats that had been specially bred to be anxious responded positively to being licked, and their anxious behavior gradually subsided under the influence of such attention. Scientists were even able to trace physical changes in the brains of these unfortunate animals, showing that grooming actually released soothing chemicals in the brain and lowered the levels of stress hormones in the body.

In all this I do not want to propose that our well-being is entirely passive or dependent on the way others treat us. Even more important than the warmth and affection we receive are the warmth and affection we give. It is through giving warmth and affection, through being genuinely concerned for others —in other words, through compassion—that we gain the conditions for genuine happiness. For this reason, loving is of even greater importance than being loved.

Many people mistakenly assume that compassion is a religious practice. This is not the case. It is true that compassion is central to the ethical teachings of all the major religious traditions, but in itself it is not a religious value. As I have said, many animals can appreciate it and certainly mammals have a capacity for it.

Many people also assume that feeling compassion for others is only good for the others and not for oneself. This is also incorrect. Whether or not our kindness brings benefit to others will depend on a great many factors, some of which will be outside our control. But whether we succeed in bringing benefit to others or not, the first beneficiary of compassion is always oneself. When compassion, or warmheartedness, arises in us and shifts our focus away from our own narrow self-interest, it is as if we open an inner door. Compassion reduces our fear, boosts our confidence, and brings us inner strength. By reducing distrust, it opens us to others and brings us a sense of connection with them and a sense of purpose and meaning in life. Compassion also gives us respite from our own difficulties.

Some time ago, while visiting Bodh Gaya, an important Buddhist pilgrimage site in India, I came down with a severe gastrointestinal infection. The pain was so intense that I was compelled to cancel the whole series of teachings I was scheduled to give there. I was very sorry to disappoint the thousands of people who had traveled to attend, many from far away. But I had to get to a hospital urgently. This meant driving through some of the poorest parts of rural India.

The discomfort in my abdomen was acute. Every time there was a bump on the road, the pain threatened to overwhelm me. Looking out the car window, I saw scenes of widespread poverty. Underfed children were running around naked in the dirt. I caught a glimpse of a very old man lying on a cot near the road. He seemed to be alone and to have no one to care for him. As the car continued on its way, I couldn't stop thinking about the tragedy of poverty and human suffering. Later I noticed that, as my thoughts had shifted away from my own suffering to contemplation of the hardships of others, my own pain had subsided.

The observation that our concern for others contributes to our own well-being is also supported by scientific research. There is now increasing scientific evidence that love, kindness, trust, and so on have not only psychological benefits but also observable benefits to physical health. I know of one recent study showing that the deliberate cultivation of love and compassion can even affect our DNA itself. An impact has been observed on the parts of our DNA known as *telomeres,* which are associated by medical science with the process of aging.

It has also been shown that negative emotions such as anxiety, anger, and resentment undermine our ability to combat illness and infection. A scientist friend recently told me that persistent negative emotions like these actually eat away at our immune system.

Years ago I attended a presentation in New York at which a medical scientist suggested that men who make disproportionately frequent use of first-person pronouns such as "I," "me," and "mine" are much more likely to suffer heart attacks than those who do not. At the time no explanation was offered, but the implication, I thought, was quite clear. Frequent use of first-person pronouns probably indicates a high level of self-focus. Such people are likely to be more prone to the stress and anxiety that accompany self-centeredness. And stress and anxiety are well known to be bad for the heart. That said, at least those who make frequent references to themselves are being honest, which in my opinion is preferable to being self-centered while pretending to be compassionate!

The inseparable relationship between mental and emotional states on the one hand and well-being and health on the other suggests to me that the very constitution of our bodies guides us toward positive emotions. As I often say, an appreciation for love and affection seems to be built into our very blood cells.

Now there is nothing inherently wrong with pursuing one's own interests. On the contrary, to do so is a natural expression of our fundamental disposition to seek happiness and to shun suffering. In fact, it is because we care for our own needs that we have the natural capacity to appreciate others' kindness and love. This instinct for self-interest becomes negative only when we are excessively self-focused. When this happens, our vision narrows, undermining our ability to see things in their wider context. And within such a narrow perspective, even small problems can create tremendous frustration and seem unbearable. In such a state, should genuinely major challenges arise, the danger is that we will lose all hope, feel desperate and alone, and become consumed with self-pity.

What is important is that when pursuing our own self-interest we should be "wise selfish" and not "foolish selfish." Being foolish selfish means pursuing our own interests in a narrow, shortsighted way. Being wise selfish means taking a broader view and recognizing that our own long-term individual interest lies in the welfare of everyone. Being wise selfish means being compassionate.

So the human capacity to care for others is not something trivial or something to be taken for granted. Rather, it is something we should cherish. Compassion is a marvel of human nature, a precious inner resource, and the foundation of our well-being and the harmony of our societies. If, therefore, we seek happiness for ourselves, we should practice compassion; and if we seek happiness for others, we should also practice compassion!

The Love of a Mother

My first teacher of compassion was my mother. She was illiterate, a simple farmer's wife, but I can think of no better example of a person profoundly imbued with the spirit of compassion. Everyone who met her was touched by her gentleness and warmheartedness. This was in contrast with my father, who was quite hot-tempered, and even smacked us children occasionally. As my mother's son, I was fortunate enough to receive a special dose of her affection, and I am sure this has helped me to be more compassionate myself. As a young child, though, I may have abused her kindness from time to time. When she used to carry me on her shoulders, I would take hold of her ears with my hands. When I wanted her to go right I would tug on her right ear. And when I wanted to go left, I would pull on her left ear. If ever she went the wrong way, I would make a great fuss. Of course, she was only pretending not to understand my signals, and she tolerated my noisy outbursts without getting cross. In fact I cannot remember my mother ever losing her temper with anyone. She was a remarkably kind person, not just to her own children, but to everyone she met.

Doubtless this love of a mother for her child is largely biological. The maternal instinct is very strong, and helps a mother overlook her own physical discomfort and exhaustion when caring for her child. This self-sacrifice has nothing to do with her level of education, her understanding of ethics, or anything else, but is quite natural.

I was reminded of the force of a mother's affection for her newborn child during a recent overnight flight between Japan and America. In the row next to mine on the airplane sat a young couple with two small children. The elder child was perhaps three or four, while the younger was still a baby, perhaps one year old. No sooner had the plane taken off than the elder child started running here and there, full of energy and excitement. The father kept going after him and bringing him back to his seat. On one occasion, I offered the boy a sweet. He took it without a word, then continued marching about. In the meantime, the younger child was crying, and the parents took turns soothing him and carrying him up and down the aisle. Eventually the older boy grew tired and settled down to sleep, but the baby continued to be restless and carried on crying. Initially the father helped tend the baby, but finally he too sat down to sleep. In the morning, I noticed that the mother's eyes were red. She had not slept, and had spent the whole night taking care of the baby, but I could detect no trace of resentment or bitterness—she was still caring for her children with great tenderness and devotion. For myself, I simply cannot imagine being so patient!

It is this kind of unconditional loving attitude—that of a mother for her newborn—that I mean when I talk about compassion as the source of all our shared ethical or spiritual values. And it is this love, which is so well shown in the Christian symbol of the Madonna and child, that I find so powerful.

Levels of Compassion

Generally I distinguish two levels of compassion. The first is the biological level I have been describing, exemplified by the affection of a mother for her newborn child. The second is an extended level, which has to be deliberately cultivated.

While compassion at the biological level can be unconditional, like the mother's love for her baby, it is also biased and limited in scope. Nevertheless, it is of the utmost importance, because it is the seed from which unbiased compassion can grow. We can take our innate capacity for warmheartedness and, using our intelligence and conviction, expand it.

Generally speaking, we have a strong tendency to reserve

our concern for those closest to us, and then to expand it to our wider community—those with whom we share language, locality, or religion, for example. This is quite natural and can be quite powerful. When people are strongly motivated by dedication to a single cause or by feelings of closeness to a particular group, they are capable of great things. Such feelings can bring people together and help them transcend their narrow self-interest. In this sense these feelings are beneficial. Unfortunately, however, such affinities—whether based on family, community, nation, language, or religion—are often accompanied by heightened discrimination between "us" and "them." The problem is that when we see ourselves only in terms of this or that group, we tend to forget about our wider identity as human beings.

A key element in biased feelings is what we can call "attachment." Once, at a scientific conference in Argentina, a mentor of my friend Francisco Varela told me that, as a scientist, he should not be too attached to his own field of research, as this might distort his ability to assess evidence objectively. Hearing these words, I immediately felt they should also apply to the religious domain. For example, as a Buddhist, I should strive not to develop excessive attachment toward Buddhism. For to do so would hinder my ability to see the value of other faith traditions.

Furthermore, when there is an element of attachment, our affection and concern for others are often dependent on the way those others relate to us. We feel concern for those who care for us and treat us well. But when our affection is dependent on the fulfillment of our own goals and expectations, which we project onto others, it will always be very fragile. So long as the others meet our expectations, everything is fine, but as soon as they do not, our feelings of affection can easily turn to resentment and even hatred.

Conversely, extended, universal compassion is not rooted in any self-regarding element, but rather in the simple awareness that all others are human beings who, just like oneself, aspire to happiness and shun suffering. With this kind of compassion, our feeling of concern for others is completely stable and unaffected by the attitude they may have toward us. Even if others threaten or verbally abuse us, our compassion for them, our concern for their welfare, remains. Genuine compassion, therefore, is directed not at people's behavior but at the people themselves.

Since resentment, anger, and animosity bring us no benefit, it is clearly in our own interests to underpin our attitude to all others with this kind of genuine unconditional and unbiased compassion. And doing so will certainly bring us benefits.

What I am calling for is that we move beyond our limited or biased sense of closeness to this or that group or identity, and instead cultivate a sense of closeness to the entire human family. The attitude of "us" and "them" can and often does lead to conflict, even war. Much better, and more realistic, is the attitude of "we."

To some, this idea of universal compassion may sound too idealistic and possibly even religious. As for its being too idealistic, I don't think it is. Many things that we now take for granted, such as the notion of universal education, would have sounded too idealistic in the past, but now are thought of as entirely practical and indeed necessary. As for the suggestion that the idea of universal compassion is religious, I disagree. Certainly, some people's selflessness and service to others are rooted in their religious devotion, such as serving God. But at the same time, there are countless others in the world today who are concerned for all humanity, and yet who do not have religion. I think of all the doctors and aid workers volunteering in places such as Darfur, Haiti, or wherever there is conflict or natural disaster. Some of them may be people of faith, but many are not. Their concern is not for this group or that group, but simply for human beings. What drives them is genuine compassion—the determination to alleviate the suffering of others.

So I have no doubt that universal compassion can be sustained within a purely secular framework. My old friend Professor Paul Ekman, a pioneer in the science of emotion, once told me that even Charles Darwin, the father of modern evolutionary theory, believed that "the love for all living creatures is the most noble attribute of man."

I remember very clearly the worldwide response to the Asian tsunami in December of 2004. The outpouring of public concern after that disaster struck me as a powerful illustration of our unity as a human family. And it was no isolated case. Similar worldwide responses of care and concern have followed more recent tragedies. In an age when news travels so fast around the world, our sense of community and our concern for those far away from us have grown enormously. In the early twentieth century, feelings of nationalism were very strong, while awareness of our entire humanity was quite weak. In those days people were less aware of what was happening in other regions or other continents. But now, with global media transmitting news at such speed, we have a deeper awareness of the interconnectedness of people everywhere. Together with this, people's concern for humanity as a whole, and their recognition of the value of basic human rights, seem to be deepening as well. To me, this trend is a source of great optimism about the future.

Having this kind of concern for all our fellow humans does not require us to be any kind of special person or saint. On the contrary, this universal compassion is within the grasp of each of us. During the Nazi dictatorship, some Germans went to great lengths to protect and save Jews, at serious risk to their own lives. When asked why they had done it, most of them answered that they had felt compelled, and that anyone would have done the same in their situation. Yet these were just ordinary people, like you and me. With compassion—a concern for fellow human beings—everyone is capable of similar acts of heroism.

Some readers may still feel resistant to the idea of universal compassion. While admiring such an outlook in others, they may feel that adopting it themselves would entail taking on "the woes of the world," and that they have no room for all this additional suffering in their lives. In a limited sense, it is true that caring for others involves sharing in hardships that are not our own. However, the discomfort that comes from sharing the pain of others is of a quite different order from the direct experience of our own suffering. When you empathize with someone who is in distress, you may initially feel some mental discomfort. But having voluntarily chosen to open yourself to the difficulties of that other person shows courage, and courage imparts confidence. By contrast, when the pain is your own, you have no such freedom or choice. The difference is clear.

Furthermore, although compassion arises from empathy, the two are not the same. Empathy is characterized by a kind of emotional resonance—feeling *with* the other person. Compassion, in contrast, is not just sharing experience with others, but also wishing to see them relieved of their suffering. Being compassionate does not mean remaining entirely at the level of feeling, which could be quite draining. After all, compassionate doctors would not be very effective if they were always preoccupied with sharing their patients' pain. Compassion means wanting to *do* something to relieve the hardships of others, and this desire to help, far from dragging us further into suffering ourselves, actually gives us energy and a sense of purpose and direction. When we *act* upon this motivation, both we and those around us benefit still more.

However, since universal compassion involves gradually expanding one's circle of concern until it finally embraces the whole of humanity, it needs constant cultivation. Using our intelligence and our conviction of its necessity and value, we gradually learn to expand and extend our concern, first to our close family, then to all those with whom we come into contact, including especially our enemies, then to our entire human family, and even to all beings.

Compassion Training

Those with religious faith have rich resources for the cultivation of compassion, and religious approaches can also be great resources for humanity as a whole. But religion is not necessary for cultivating compassion. In fact, secular techniques for compassion training are already in use, and their effectiveness has even been scientifically demonstrated. It seems that developing inner values is much like physical exercise. The more we train our abilities, the stronger they become. Neuroscientific research conducted by my old friend Professor Richard Davidson, for example, has demonstrated that even short periods of compassion training—as brief as two weeks—can lead to observable changes in the patterns of the brain, as well as to a greater inclination toward charitable giving. I am hopeful that such research may pave the way for the introduction of compassion training in schools, which could be very worthwhile. Modern education is premised strongly on materialistic values. Yet, as I often point out, it is vital that when educating our children's brains we do not neglect to educate their hearts, and a key element of educating their hearts has to be nurturing their compassionate nature. This is a subject to which I will return.

5

Compassion and the Question of Justice

The Question of Justice

ON A NUMBER of recent occasions, thoughtful people who are sympathetic to the idea of secular ethics have objected to my suggestion that compassion can be the foundation of such a secular system. For many, it seems, there is a conflict between the principle of compassion, which implies forgiveness, and the exercise of justice, which requires punishment for wrongdoing. As they see it, the principle of justice or fairness, rather than that of compassion, must underpin any humanistic approach to ethics. To give priority to compassion and forgiveness, they argue, would allow perpetrators of harm to go unpunished and hand victory to the aggressors. The ethic of compassion, they say, amounts to little more than an ethic of victimhood, under which aggression always triumphs, wrongdoing is always forgiven, and the weak are defenseless.

This objection rests, in my view, on a fundamental misunderstanding of what compassion entails in practice. Nothing in the principle of compassion—the wish to see others relieved of suffering—involves surrendering to the misdeeds of others. Nor does compassion demand that we meekly accept injustice.

Far from promoting weakness or passivity, compassion requires great fortitude and strength of character.

Some of the greatest fighters against injustice of recent times, people of strong character and determination like Mahatma Gandhi, Mother Teresa, Nelson Mandela, Martin Luther King Jr., Václav Havel, and others—have been motivated by universal compassion. One could not describe such people as meek or retiring just because they combined their devotion to the welfare of others with a commitment to nonviolence.

As I have said, compassion by no means implies surrender in the face of wrongdoing or injustice. When an unjust situation demands a strong response, as in the case of apartheid, compassion demands, not that we accept injustice, but that we take a stand against it. It does imply that such a stand should be nonviolent. But nonviolence is not a sign of weakness, but rather one of self-confidence and courage. Generally, when people quarrel, it is only when they run out of arguments that they lose their tempers and resort to shouting and even violence. But when parties to a dispute feel confident that truth is on their side, often they remain calm and continue to argue their case. So maintaining an attitude of calmness and nonviolence is actually an indication of strength, as it shows the confidence that comes from having truth and justice on one's side.

We might illustrate this point, about the need to stand up to injustice while maintaining a compassionate concern for the wrongdoer, with an example at a personal level. Imagine yourself with difficult neighbors, who repeatedly behave aggressively toward you. What is the appropriate compassionate response? In my understanding, there is no reason why compassion, including of course compassion toward the aggressors, should prevent you from making a forceful response. Depending on the context, a failure to respond with strong measures, thereby allowing the aggressors to continue their destructive behavior, could even make you partially responsible for the harm they continue to inflict. In addition, doing nothing to oppose such behavior in effect encourages those unfortunate persons, with the likely consequence that they will move on to even more destructive behavior, bringing still greater harm to others and, in the long run, to themselves. The only way to change a person's mind is with concern, not with anger or hatred. Physical or violent measures can only restrain others' physical behavior, never their minds.

There is a story from southern Tibet about a person who tells a friend, "Such and such person hit me once, I kept quiet; he hit me twice, I kept quiet; he hit me three times, I kept quiet; he kept hitting me, still I kept quiet." This is an illustration of what compassion is not. This is meekness, and it is not the right way. What is required in the face of injustice is strong compassion!

Broad and Narrow Concepts of Justice

So there is no conflict between compassion, correctly understood, and the exercise of justice. In saying this, however, it is important to distinguish between the general principle of justice—as a universal precept of fairness and redress based on the recognition of human equality—and the narrower understanding of justice as the exercise of the law within any given legal framework. Ideally, these two conceptions of justice should always reflect one another, but sometimes, unfortunately, they do not. If we consider South Africa under apartheid rule, it is apparent that a judicial system can ignore the universal principle of human equality, and instead protect the interests of a particular section of society. During that time, a nonwhite person could be punished for infringing the interests of the ruling minority, even in trivial matters. A similar situation prevailed in India under colonial rule and continues to do so in other parts of the world, wherever specific minorities and groups are suppressed by others. Clearly such legal systems reflect a very limited conception of justice.

There are also situations in which the rights of one religious community or political group are constrained by another. When a country's legal system enshrines national unity and social order as its highest priorities, and deems any actions construed as undermining these values as criminal offenses, that legal system will not serve genuine justice. The long imprisonment of Aung San Suu Kyi after her election victory in Burma is an example of this. And the recent arrest of my fellow Nobel Peace Laureate Liu Xiaobo in China is another. When people criticize such violations of justice, countries defend themselves by saying everything has been done according to the rule of law. However, when the law is tied to narrow interests, it fails to uphold the fundamental conception of justice as a principle of fairness based on human equality. For the law genuinely to uphold justice, it must protect universal human rights.

The Role of Punishment

Of course, most of us recognize justice as a universal principle of fairness based on our fundamental equality as human beings—whether equality before God, equality in terms of our basic aspiration to happiness and the avoidance of suffering, or equality before the law as citizens. Yet it seems there is less consensus concerning the actual exercise of justice in matters of crime and punishment. For example, people disagree about issues such as the death penalty and the purpose of punishment. Some feel that certain crimes are so heinous, so negative, that their perpetrators should be shown no mercy.

When it comes to wrongdoing, all the major religions have some idea of redress or of restoring the balance in the life or lives to come. In the theistic traditions, there is the understanding that there will be a divine judgment. In traditional Buddhist teaching, the law of karma ensures that individuals will eventually experience the fruits of their actions. Both of these beliefs allow mercy to be shown in worldly human affairs. From a secular point of view, without such beliefs in punishment and reward in the afterlife, we must ask ourselves what punishment is really about. Is it about retribution and revenge—about making wrongdoers suffer as an end in itself? Or is it more about preventing further wrongdoing? To my mind, the purpose of punishment is not to exact suffering as an end in itself. Rather, the suffering inflicted by punishment should have a higher purpose, namely to discourage the wrongdoer from repeating the offense and to deter others from committing similar acts. Punishment is, therefore, not about retribution but about deterrence.

Of course, courts of law must have at their disposal the means to punish wrongdoers. To leave terrible crimes such as murder and violent assault unpunished would be to suggest that the worst potentialities of humanity are somehow acceptable, and this would not be in the interests of anyone, including the perpetrators of such crimes themselves. Punishment has an inevitable and important role to play in the regulation of human affairs, both as a deterrent and to give people a sense of security and confidence in the law.

However, if punishment were about deterrence alone, then it might be argued that even minor acts of wrongdoing should receive very severe punishments, as the most effective deterrent against such behavior. While this might be a way of ensuring low rates of crime, it is not an approach I can accept. It cannot be just to punish someone very severely for a minor misdeed. Instead there should be some idea of proportionality: the more severe the offense, the more severe the punishment.

But this raises the question, What are the limits of redress? Here I think it is very important to recognize that all human beings have the capacity for change. Because of this, I find the idea of the death penalty unacceptable. This is why, for many years, I have supported Amnesty International's campaign for its abolition. My view is not a matter of leniency. But to kill other human beings in retribution, no matter what they have done, cannot to my mind be right, since it forecloses the possibility that they may change. I believe it is wiser for a society to keep that possibility available.

Now, I understand that violent retribution—reacting aggressively to an assault, for example—is something quite deeply rooted in human instinct. In this we are not unlike other animals, which, when challenged, may even fight to the death. But the exercise of vengeance seems to be a particularly human trait, one related to our capacity to remember. In primitive human society, revenge may have been necessary for survival, but as society developed, people came to recognize the negative consequences of revenge and the value of forgiveness. This, I think, is what it really means to be civilized.

So I believe that to indulge our violent instincts by pursuing revenge is misguided and not in anyone's best interests. For the only guaranteed result of vengeance is that it will sow the seeds of further conflict. It stirs up resentment and with it the danger of an escalating cycle of violence and retaliation which can only be broken when the principle of vengeance is itself discarded. Indulging a craving for revenge creates an atmosphere of fear, further resentment, and hatred. By contrast, where there is forgiveness there is the chance of peace. Therefore, in my understanding, revenge has no place in the exercise of justice. The very idea is outdated. For while revenge weakens society, forgiveness gives it strength.

This was powerfully illustrated by what happened in South Africa after the dismantling of the apartheid system. Under Nelson Mandela's wise leadership, the African National Congress acted with magnanimity to ensure that there were almost no incidents of revenge against the minority white community. Had the leaders instead chosen to dwell on the past and created a climate of resentment, the situation could have been truly tragic. Instead, the government established the Truth and Reconciliation Commission, headed by my old friend and spiritual colleague Archbishop Desmond Tutu. Following his moral example, the commission operated on the principle that the expression of truth by those responsible for serious wrongdoing, even atrocities, would have a healing and liberating effect for both the victims and the perpetrators of these crimes. Today, more than ten years after the commission finished its work, there can be little doubt that the process brought peace of mind and closure to a great many people, both victims and violators. I had the great honor to meet President Mandela soon after South Africa obtained its freedom from apartheid. I was greatly impressed, not only by his gracefulness but also by his total absence of resentment toward those responsible for his long imprisonment.

To my mind there is no doubt that the exercise of justice, far from being at odds with the principle of compassion, should be informed by a compassionate approach. I always remember the justice minister of Scotland's explanation of his difficult decision to release the man convicted of the Lockerbie airplane bombing. In his country, he said, people "desire justice and want justice to be tempered by compassion and mercy." I am aware that his decision caused a great deal of controversy and anger among some of the victims' families. Nonetheless, I think the minister's statement was in itself very sound. When it comes to justice, compassion and mercy should not be brushed aside.

Distinguishing the Action from the Actor

The important point about the principle of compassion, as a basis for the exercise of justice, is that it is directed not toward *actions,* but toward the *actor.* Compassion demands that we condemn wrong actions and oppose them with all means necessary, while at the same time forgiving and maintaining an attitude of kindness toward the perpetrators of those actions. Just as, in theistic terms, God forbids sin while still loving the sinner, so we too should forcefully oppose wrong while maintaining concern for the wrongdoer. It is right to do this because, again, all human beings are capable of change. I think we all know this from our own experience. After all, it is not uncommon for those who lead reckless lives when young to become responsible and caring as they gain in maturity and experience. In history, too, there are many examples of individuals whose early lives were morally reprehensible, but who later brought great benefit to others. We might think of Emperor Ashoka, for example, or Saint Paul, or numerous others.

This capacity for change is true even of those who have committed the most terrible deeds. I am encouraged in this belief by my discussions over the years with prisoners' representatives and social workers involved with prisons both in India and the United States. It is a great tragedy that, in many countries, as statistics suggest, a majority of prisoners later reoffend. Some countries are now introducing rehabilitation programs which offer offenders guidance on how they can, through mental training, gradually readjust their understanding of the world and learn to contribute to rather than detract from the well-being of others. For example, under an initiative introduced by Kiran Bedi in Delhi's high-security Tihar jail, prisoners are given classes in mindfulness meditation. I am optimistic that, with time, this program will prove effective in helping even the most desperate inmates develop a sense of purpose in life through concern for others. I am always humbled when I meet the people who run such programs and the prisoners who have felt their positive impact.

To summarize, let me say simply: Remember that even a criminal is a human being, like yourself, and capable of change. Punish the actor in proportion to the misdeed, but do not indulge the desire for vengeance. Think rather of the future, and of how to ensure that the crime is not repeated.

Altruistic Punishment

Not long ago, I attended a conference in Zurich on the subject of compassion and altruism in economic systems. At the conference, an Austrian economist named Ernst Fehr introduced an interesting concept that he calls "altruistic punishment."

He illustrated the concept by means of a game of trust. The game is played in rounds and involves ten players. The players are given equal amounts of money and asked to contribute some of it to a collective fund. The experimenter explains that in each round the total amount the players contribute to this fund will be doubled and then redistributed equally among them. In the early rounds, most players are quite generous, making substantial contributions to the central fund, in the belief that others will do the same. This, I think, reflects the intuitively optimistic side of human nature. Inevitably, however, there are some individuals who hold back and contribute nothing. In basic monetary terms, they see that what profits them most is to keep their share of what is given, without spending any money of their own. Such people, I understand, are known in the language of economics as "free riders." As a result of their behavior, the other players start to feel they are being taken advantage of, and begin to contribute less and less to the central fund until finally, usually by about the tenth round, the entire system breaks down. At this stage, no one is willing to contribute, even though the experimenter's offer to double any money contributed is still in place.

At this point the players are introduced to the notion of altruistic punishment, a mechanism by which they can punish the free riders. By contributing some of their own money to a nonrefundable punishment bin, they are able to force free riders to pay double that amount. So, for example, by spending three dollars on punishment, a player can make the free rider pay six dollars. As it turns out, once this system is introduced into the game, cooperation between players can be sustained more or less indefinitely. Would-be free riders are deterred from taking advantage of others, and as a result the players continue to contribute to the central fund and everyone benefits.

Although this experiment was principally designed to test a theory in economics, I feel that it also contains a universally applicable message. It shows us that punishment can be exacted in a way which benefits everyone, including wrongdoers themselves. It illustrates the point that punishment which does not exact revenge, but rather corrects the wrongdoer, is in everyone's interest.

Forgiveness

Forgiveness is an essential part of a compassionate attitude, but it is a virtue that is easily misunderstood. For a start, to forgive is not the same as to forget. After all, if one forgets a wrong that has been done, there is nothing left to forgive! Instead, what I am suggesting is that we find a way of dealing with wrongdoing that gives us peace of mind and at the same time keeps us from succumbing to destructive impulses like the desire for revenge. I will say more about ways in which we can do this later on, but part of what is required is an acceptance that what is done is done. Whether at the level of the individual or at the level of society as a whole, it is important to acknowledge that the past is beyond our control. The way we *respond* to past wrongdoing is not, however.

As I have already mentioned, it is vital to keep in mind the distinction between the doer and the deed. Sometimes this can be hard. When we ourselves or those very close to us have been victims of terrible crimes, it can be difficult not to feel hatred toward the perpetrators of those crimes. And yet, if we pause to think about it, we realize that distinguishing between a terrible deed and its perpetrator is actually something we do every day with regard to our own actions and our own transgressions. In moments of anger or irritation, we may be rude to loved ones or aggressive toward others. Later we may feel some remorse or regret, but when looking back on our outburst, we do not fail to distinguish between what we *did* and who we *are*. We naturally forgive ourselves and perhaps resolve not to do the same thing again. Given that we find it so easy to forgive ourselves, surely we can extend the same courtesy to others! Of course not everyone is able to forgive him- or herself, and this can be an obstacle. For such people, it may be important to practice compassion and forgiveness toward themselves, as the foundation for practicing compassion and forgiveness toward others.

Another truth to keep in mind is that forgiving others has an enormously liberating effect on oneself. When you dwell on the harm someone has done to you, there is an inevitable tendency to become angry and resentful at the thought. Yet clinging to painful memories and harboring ill will will do nothing to rectify the wrong committed and will have no positive effect on you. Your peace of mind will be destroyed, your sleep will be disturbed, and eventually even your physical health is likely to suffer. If, on the other hand, you are able to overcome your feelings of hostility toward wrongdoers and forgive them, there is an immediate and perceptible benefit to you. By leaving past actions in the past and restoring your concern for the well-being of those who have done you wrong, you gain a tremendous feeling of inner confidence and freedom, which allows you to move on as your negative thoughts and emotions tend to dissipate.

For me, the power of forgiveness is strikingly apparent in the example of a man I consider a personal hero, Richard Moore. In 1972, at just ten years old, Richard was completely blinded by a rubber bullet fired by a British soldier in Northern Ireland. The tragedy could have turned the boy into an angry and resentful man. But Richard never bore ill will, and he devoted his life to the positive cause of helping and protecting other vulnerable children around the world. In fact, he made it his business to find the man who had blinded him and tell him he was forgiven. The two men are now friends. What a marvelous example of the power of compassion and forgiveness!

Though we Tibetans have suffered a great deal, still, as a people, we try to refrain from succumbing to any tendency for hostility and revenge. Even toward the Chinese communist soldiers responsible for atrocities against Tibetans, we try to maintain compassion. Sometimes this produces unexpected results. Recently, for example, I met the son of a Chinese cavalry officer who, as a member of the People's Liberation Army in the late 1950s, was involved in the persecution of Tibetans. The father, now old, had sent me a message through his son offering regret and sincere apologies for his deeds. To hear this was most moving. Yet I think that, had there been hatred on my part, this incident would only have served to increase it. By not clinging to past experiences of injustice, by consciously trying to develop compassion toward our Chinese brothers and sisters, we Tibetans avoid being stuck in the past and can maintain a sense of freedom. But this does not mean that we do not stand firm against the injustices we face.

So in answer to those who insist that justice, rather than compassion, should lie at the heart of any system of ethics, I suggest that in reality there is no conflict between the principle of justice and the practice of compassion and forgiveness. Indeed, in my understanding the very concept of justice is itself based on compassion.

The Scope of Ethics

In conclusion, it is worth briefly exploring the scope of ethics. If ethics is understood only as a mechanism for maintaining social order, then it will cover only those aspects of outward human behavior which have a direct and observable impact on others. And if it only relates to the impact of our actions on others—in effect, to the *consequences* of our actions—then whatever feelings and intentions we may harbor in our hearts will be irrelevant or neutral with regard to ethics. But this I cannot accept. This understanding of ethics is much too narrow.

The very notion of ethics makes no sense without a consideration of motivation. If we bumped our head on a tree, would we blame the tree? Of course we would not! The idea of moral responsibility presupposes the presence of some inner motivation. So, to me, to describe ethics without reference to the level of motivation seems very incomplete.

In fact, the inner motivational dimension is the most important aspect of ethics. For when our motivation is pure, genuinely directed toward the benefit of others, our actions will naturally tend to be ethically sound. This is why I consider compassion to be the core principle on which an entire ethical approach can be built. It is from a compassionate concern for the welfare of others that all our ethical values and principles arise, including that of justice.

6

The Role of Discernment

UNTIL NOW I have emphasized the importance of compassion—a motivation of genuine concern for others' welfare—as the foundation of ethics and spiritual well-being and even the basis for understanding justice. Recognizing our shared humanity and our biological nature as beings whose happiness is dependent on others, we learn to open our hearts, and in so doing we gain a sense of purpose and of connection with those around us. Broad, unbiased compassion, I have also suggested, is the ground from which all positive inner values—patience, kindness, forgiveness, self-discipline, contentment, and so on—emerge.

However, while sound compassionate motivation is the foundation of ethics and spirituality, a further factor is crucial if we are to achieve a balanced and genuinely universal system of ethics. While intention is the first and most important factor in guaranteeing that our behavior is ethical, we also need *discernment* to ensure that the choices we make are realistic and that our good intentions do not go to waste.

If, for example, politicians take their country to war without having fully considered the likely consequences, then even if their motivation is sincerely compassionate, the outcome is likely to be disastrous. What is required, therefore, in addition to good intention, is the use of our critical faculty, our discernment. The exercise of discernment, which enables us to relate to situations in a manner that is in tune with reality, enables us to translate our good intentions into good outcomes.

Discernment also plays a crucial role in generating our own personal level of ethical awareness. Using our intelligence is the way we come to understanding, and understanding is the basis of awareness. So ethical awareness—that is to say, awareness of what will benefit both oneself and others—does not arise magically, but comes from the use of reason. In this, education in ethical awareness is no different from any other kind of education.

Establishing Inner Values

All of our actions have consequences, and these inevitably have an impact on both ourselves and others. Since in everyday life we constantly have to make small decisions which have this ethical dimension, it is very helpful to have basic ethical rules or guidelines to fall back on. Even the choice of which products to buy or what food to eat involves some ethical discernment. When making such choices we generally do not have the opportunity to think through all the options available and reflect on all probable consequences on a case-by-case basis. In fact, if we were to reflect deeply on every single ethical choice we face, I don't think we would have much time left for anything else. For those occasions when we do not have time to work things out in detail, it is useful to have internalized general rules to guide our actions.

The major religions of the world are all rich in such guidelines, and when these rules are inculcated from an early age, they become part of a person's internal value system. For example, in traditional Tibetan society, the Buddhist principle of avoidance of causing harm to animals was a value that people acquired from the cultural environment. From a young age, children were taught to avoid killing even insects, so this avoidance became internalized and automatic. If they accidentally happened to step on an insect, they would say, "*Akha, nyingje*" (Oh, the poor thing!). In Tibet in the past there was actually legislation banning hunting and fishing, except in a few areas where people's livelihood depended on these activities. There were also more specific laws protecting wildlife, such as regulations concerning the migrating birds that nest around Manasarovar and other lakes. Paid rangers ensured that their eggs were not disturbed. These regulations are examples of the ways the prevailing culture helps to form people's ethical priorities.

But in a purely secular context, although people of course still have ingrained values, what these are cannot always be taken for granted. Some actions, such as killing, stealing, lying, slander, and sexual exploitation—all of which are forms of violence—are by definition harmful to others, so most people instinctively feel the value of avoiding them. But we need to go further than this in a globalized world in which religious moral guidelines are not universally accepted. We need to use our discernment to gain understanding about the benefits of certain kinds of behavior and the negative consequences of other kinds.

In this way, we can develop an internalized value system to guide us in our responses to everyday life.

What is therefore required is that we reflect on our behavior, using our discernment to assess which of our actions are most harmful to ourselves and to others and which are most beneficial. In so doing, we can gradually learn to identify those aspects of our conduct which need to be curbed and those which need to be cultivated.

For example, by using our discernment to consider the consequences of violence, we can gradually reach a clear understanding and conviction of its harmfulness and futility. Similarly, by using our discernment to reflect on the consequences of patience or generosity, we can come to understand their positive effects, and we can nurture this understanding so that it becomes a deeply engrained part of our awareness. When this happens we will find that our behavior is spontaneously more oriented toward the well-being of others. This kind of mental training is a theme to which I will return in the second part of the book.

Dealing with Dilemmas

While internalized values are indispensable as practical tools for living ethically, there are, unfortunately, exceptional circumstances in which such general principles are inadequate. Particular situations may present themselves in which we are forced to choose between principles we hold dear. It is in such cases that the use of discernment, in service of our compassionate motivation, becomes crucial. For only by assessing the probable consequences and weighing the pros and cons of different courses of action can we come to a balanced conclusion about which course of action is most beneficial.

In my own case, when called upon to make a difficult decision, I always start by checking my motivation. Do I truly have others' well-being at heart? Am I under the sway of any disturbing emotions, such as anger, impatience, or hostility? Having determined that my motivation is sound, I then look carefully at the situation in context. What are the underlying causes and conditions that have given rise to it? What choices do I have? What are their likely outcomes? And which course of action, on balance, is most likely to yield the greatest long-term benefit for others? Making decisions in this way, I find, means they are not the cause of any regret later on.

So while I encourage the reader to internalize a personal value system, it would be unrealistic to suppose that matters of ethics can be determined purely on the basis of rules and precepts. Matters of ethics are often not black and white. After checking to be sure that we are motivated by concern for the welfare of humanity, we must weigh the pros and the cons of the various paths open to us and then let ourselves be guided by a natural sense of responsibility. This, essentially, is what it means to be wise.

Taking a Holistic View

Discernment is crucial if we are to have a realistic understanding of the world we live in. Here the key principle we need to grasp is that of *interdependence.* This general yet profound principle can be approached at various levels and in various contexts. It is worth careful consideration. We have already discussed the interdependence of our own well-being and that of others; in addition, interdependence is a characteristic of the world which is apparent in many fields. We might consider interdependence in global finance or economics, or the interdependence of humanity itself in an age of globalization, or interdependence in the natural world, which biologists discuss in terms of "food chains" and "symbiosis" between living organisms. And in the challenging field of quantum physics, with its notions of "general relativity" and "quantum entanglement," there is interdependence even in theories of the origin of the universe. Recognizing that so many aspects of our world are characterized by relations of mutual dependence can help us form a more realistic understanding of the world—an understanding that is more in keeping with the way things actually are.

Every situation we face in life arises from the convergence of a great number of contributing factors, so taking a broad view is essential if our responses are to be realistic. It is not enough to look at any given situation or problem from only one perspective. We need to look at it from this direction and that direction, from all sides. As I often say, we should look from front and back, the two dimensions; from the right side and the left side, four dimensions; and from above and below, making six dimensions. When we do this, when we take this kind of broader or more holistic perspective, our responses will definitely be more in tune with reality. And with this, we are more likely to achieve our objectives.

Often, when problems arise, people have an unfortunate tendency to view them from too narrow a perspective. For example, imagine that your car won't start. For you to keep turning the key again and again, becoming frustrated and running the battery down, would be foolish. It would more realistic to pause and consider what might have caused the problem. Could it be a lack of fuel, or something to do with the rainy weather? Simply stepping back and looking at the situation from a broader perspective will allow you to approach the problem more calmly. Needless to say, this will also give you a better chance of being able to deal with the problem efficiently.

Again, when misfortune befalls us, our tendency is to see it as the consequence of a single cause and rush to blame others. But this kind of overly emotional response is actually quite unrealistic. When the bus is late, what benefit do we gain from getting angry with the driver? Very often, the actions of any single person play only a minor role in the way events unfold. Responding to setbacks with accusations and blame—whether directed at others or at oneself—is generally misguided, and very likely will only worsen the situation. The fact is, every incident we encounter comes about as the result of countless different causes and conditions, many of which are beyond any individual's control, and some of which may even remain hidden altogether.

So in the face of a major challenge, such as losing a job, we may become paralyzed by anxiety, locked onto the negative aspects of what has happened, thinking, "Now I won't be able to support my family," and "Poor me, I'll never get another job."

The danger of this attitude is that by focusing too narrowly on our immediate predicament, we will find ourselves unable to do anything about it. In contrast, using our discernment to look at situations in their broader context and from different perspectives will help us find solutions.

Inevitable Uncertainty

Of course, no matter how hard we may try, human discernment is always incomplete. Unless we are clairvoyant or omniscient, like Buddha or like God, we will never see the entire picture, and we will never know all the causes that have given rise to any situation. Nor can we foresee all the consequences of our actions. There is always bound to be some element of uncertainty. It is important to acknowledge this, but it should not worry us. Still less should it make us despair of the value of rational assessment. Instead it should temper our actions with proper humility and caution. Sometimes, admitting that we do not know an answer can be helpful in itself. If we do not know something, it is better to admit it openly than to feign certainty out of misplaced pride or vanity.

This uncertainty is another reason why ethics must be grounded at the level of motivation, as I have said, rather than purely on consideration of consequences. The fact is, the consequences of our actions are often not within our control. Where we do have control is at the level of motivation and in deploying our critical faculties, our discernment. When we combine these two elements, we can ensure that we are doing our best.

The Fruits of Discernment

All the uses of discernment outlined above give us understanding, and reflection on that understanding gives us a deeper and more enduring awareness. When discernment is combined with a compassionate motivation, we have the two key components of a comprehensive approach to ethics and spiritual well-being in a secular context. And these two components—compassion and discernment—are mutually reinforcing. Compassion, by reducing fear and distrust, creates a space in our hearts and minds that is calm and settled, and this space makes it much easier for us to exercise discernment or intelligence. Similarly, the exercise of discernment can strengthen our conviction of the necessity and the benefits of compassion. The two, therefore, complement each other in a profound way.

7

Ethics in Our Shared World

Our Global Challenges

AT MY RESIDENCE in Dharamsala, the hill station in northern India which has been my home since the early 1960s, it is my daily habit to rise early, normally at around 3:30 A.M. After some hours of mental exercises and contemplation, I generally listen to the world news on the radio. Most often, I tune in to the BBC World Service. It is a routine I have followed for many years, as a way of staying in touch with events around the world.

As I listen to the constant stream of reports about money and finance, about crises, conflicts, and war, it often strikes me that the complex problems we face in the world—problems of corruption, environment, politics, and so on—almost always indicate a failure of moral ethics and inner values. At every level we see a lack of self-discipline. Many problems are also due to failures of discernment, of shortsightedness or narrow-mindedness.

Of course the causes and conditions of particular problems can be immensely complex. The seeds of ethnic violence, rebellion, and war, for example, almost invariably date back decades or even centuries. But still, if we are really interested in tackling our problems at their roots—whether we are talking about human conflict, poverty, or environmental destruction—we have to recognize that they are ultimately related to issues of ethics. Our shared problems do not fall from the sky, nor are they created by some higher force. For the most part, they are products of human action and human error. If human action can create these problems in the first place, then surely we humans must have the capacity as well as the responsibility to find their solutions. The only way we can put them right is by changing our outlook and our ways, and by taking action.

Global Responsibility

Occasionally I notice that people are making a convenient distinction between ethics on the personal level and ethics on the wider social level. To me, such attitudes are fundamentally flawed, as they overlook the interdependence of our world.

That individual ethics—or rather their absence—can have an impact on the lives of many is powerfully demonstrated by the global financial crisis that began in 2008, the repercussions of which are still being felt around the world. It revealed the way unbridled greed on the part of a few can adversely affect the lives of millions. So, just as in the wake of the 9/11 attacks we started to take the dangers of religious extremism and intolerance seriously, so too, in the wake of the financial crisis, should we take the dangers of greed and dishonesty seriously. When greed is seen as acceptable, even praiseworthy, there is clearly something wrong with our collective value system.

In this age of globalization, the time has come for us to acknowledge that our lives are deeply interconnected and to recognize that our behavior has a global dimension. When we do so, we will see that our own interests are best served by what is in the best interests of the wider human community. By contrast, if we concentrate exclusively on our inner development and neglect the wider problems of the world, or if, having recognized these, we are apathetic about trying to solve them, then we have overlooked something fundamental. Apathy, in my view, is itself a form of selfishness. For our approach to ethics to be truly meaningful, we must of course care about the world. This is what I mean by the principle of global responsibility, which is a key part of my approach to secular ethics.

The Challenge of Technological Progress

With the colossal scientific and technological advances—military, medical, and agricultural—of the past two centuries, humans now have unprecedented knowledge of, and power over, the world. Never before have we known so much, or been in such a position of control over so many aspects of our planet. This situation raises a very serious concern: Is it possible that our responsibilities are now growing too fast for our natural capacity for moral discernment to keep pace? Can we trust ourselves with the power that science and technology have brought us? While our brains have not changed appreciably in the past five thousand years, the world around us has changed to an extraordinary degree.

Despite today's global challenges, I remain broadly optimistic. Time and again, we humans have risen to the challenges we have faced. We have successfully navigated many transitions in the course of our evolution from communities of hunter-gatherers to high-tech urban societies. This in itself is powerful testimony to our resilience and resourcefulness as social and moral creatures. In fact, despite all the wars, disasters, and diseases we have encountered, the human race not only survives but thrives. Far from destroying ourselves, we have in fact created an opposite problem—a human population rising at an unprecedented and alarming rate.

Our success as a species has been made possible by our ability, particularly when our vital interests are threatened, to *cooperate.* And at the very heart of cooperation is the principle of taking into account the interests and welfare of others. I am therefore confident that we humans will once again find ways, through cooperation, to overcome our current ecological and technological challenges. But there can be no room for complacency.

The Futility of War

The twentieth century was one of intense human conflict on a scale never seen before. It is estimated that more than two hundred million people were killed in wars, revolutions, and genocides. From the Nazi holocaust to the mass murder by despots such as Stalin and Mao (in the later part of his career); from the killing fields of the Khmer Rouge to the attempts at ethnic cleansing in the Balkans and the genocide in Rwanda, the suffering that humanity has inflicted upon itself is truly hard to bear.

Of course, human history has always been interrupted by war. So long as there are humans, I think there will always be some conflict—but the scale of destruction in the past hundred years has been unprecedented.

Even during times of peace, human technologies of destruction have been developed, enhanced, and traded without pause. Today there is no place on the face of the earth unthreatened by these arsenals of destruction. When approaching the problem of violence in the world and thinking about how we can create a safer world for future generations, we must do more than just appeal to politicians and their adversaries to exercise restraint. The threats we live with also stem from the weapons industry itself, from the arms trade, and indeed from the culture of violence—often perpetuated by the media—which encourages the delusion that violence is a viable approach to resolving human conflict. Really what we need is a fundamental shift in human awareness. For in all but the most exceptional circumstances, violence only begets further violence. To suppose that we can achieve peace through violence is therefore altogether misguided.

In the contemporary, deeply interdependent world, war is outdated and illogical. When, in the distant past, the interests of two groups were entirely separate, violence as a last resort may have had some justification. But this is not the case today. All regions and all peoples are connected environmentally, economically, and politically. War, oppression, or civil strife in one area inevitably affects people in other parts of the world. The problem of terrorism is an extreme example. When people are powerfully motivated toward destruction, no policing or security system will ever be adequate to prevent them.

A further factor which makes violence an unrealistic means for resolving conflict is the unpredictability of its outcomes. The recent war in Iraq is a good example. Though the initial intention was to conduct a limited campaign, the result was a protracted and as yet unresolved conflict which has devastated the lives of millions of innocent people.

In the remaining years of the twenty-first century, we must ensure that we do not repeat the mistakes of the past. The only way to reduce the level of violence in our world is for more and more people across the globe to consciously adopt a stance of disarmament. Disarmament is compassion in practice. What is required, therefore, is both inner disarmament, at the level of our individual hatred, prejudice, and intolerance, and outer disarmament, at the level of nations and states. Rather than pouring salt on the wounds we have inherited from earlier generations, we must start to heal our divisions by committing ourselves to dialogue, cooperation, and understanding. As the population of the globe continues to grow, and as large nations like China, India, and Brazil race ahead with rapid economic expansion, global competition for natural resources—not just fossil fuels but also basic necessities like water, food, and land—will inevitably intensify. So it is vital that our younger generations, the guardians of our future, develop strong awareness of the futility of war. We can learn from the great achievements of Mahatma Gandhi and Martin Luther King Jr. to recognize that nonviolence is the best long-term approach to redressing injustice. If the twentieth century was a century of violence, let us make the twenty-first a century of dialogue.

The Environment

For several decades I have emphasized the importance of environmental awareness to our future well-being. It is most encouraging that in recent years such awareness has been increasing, especially among the young, and that politicians are now having to take these issues seriously.

In the past, when industrialization began in Europe and gradually spread to other parts of the globe, the complex interrelationships of the natural world were poorly understood. In the name of progress, animals were hunted to extinction, forests were cut down, and waterways were polluted by factories and industrial plants. But as science has advanced and our understanding of the delicate balance of the natural world has grown, the excuse of ignorance is no longer available.

Today, we must face the reality that our excessively materialistic lifestyles are wasteful and come at a considerable environmental cost. It is only natural for people in the developing world to aspire to the same level of comfort enjoyed by those in the developed world. But with the global population rising rapidly, it is clear that if we do not change the patterns of consumption we consider "advanced," humanity's thirst for natural resources will be unsustainable. Already we are seeing the results: overexploitation and the corresponding degradation of the natural environment are generating environmental crises at local and global levels. It is very important, therefore, that the nations which are pursuing such rapid economic growth do not blindly follow the models of development they see in the more affluent countries. Instead, countries such as China, India, and Brazil should take the lead in finding new, more sustainable avenues of development. In this regard I consider the economic model of microfinance, which can be flexible and sensitive to local and environmental issues, to be very forward-thinking.

The challenges posed by the environment require cooperation at a global level. Climate change is a clear example. In Tibet, which some environmentalists call the "Third Pole" because its glaciers are so important in the weather systems of Asia, deglaciation is already being observed, and the temperature on the Tibetan plateau is reportedly increasing at a considerably faster rate than that in adjacent lowland areas. Many of Asia's most important rivers—the Yangtze and Yellow Rivers, the Mekong, the Salween, the Brahmaputra, and the Indus, for example—rise in Tibet. As the glaciers recede, all the areas downstream will become more vulnerable to drought. This will come in addition to the effects of deforestation, which is already taking its toll in greater levels of flooding. In the long run, deglaciation in Tibet could contribute to drastic climate change and severe water shortages and desertification in China, India, Pakistan, and Southeast Asia. This would be catastrophic for the whole world.

It is no longer realistic for states to think only of their narrow national self-interest. Developed nations, which enjoy so many benefits, must act in cooperation with developing nations, which naturally want to share those benefits. Genuine cooperation cannot, however, be imposed by force; it can only emerge from mutual trust and respect among the parties involved, and trust comes only with transparency. The failure of the 2009 Copenhagen Summit on the global environment was, sadly, an example of how, when parties fail to look beyond their own narrow self-interest, cooperation becomes impossible.

The Problem of Greed Versus the Joys of Philanthropy

In today's materialistic world there is a trend of people becoming slaves to money, as though they are parts of a huge money-making machine. This does nothing for human dignity, freedom, and genuine well-being. Wealth should serve humanity, and not vice versa. The massive disparities of wealth now apparent in the world, disparities that are more extreme than ever before and are still growing, are very distressing. The stark economic inequalities of today's world, not just between the global north and the global south, but between rich and poor within individual nations, are not only morally wrong but sources of many practical problems, including war, sectarian violence, and the social tensions created by large-scale economic migration. On the issue of economic inequality, I consider myself at least half Marxist. When it comes to creating wealth and thereby improving people's material conditions, capitalism is without doubt very effective, but capitalism is clearly inadequate as any kind of social ideal, since it is only motivated by profit, without any ethical principle guiding it. Unbridled capitalism can involve terrible exploitation of the weak. Thus we need to adopt an approach to economic justice which respects the dynamism of capitalism while combining it with a concern for the less fortunate. Once again, I think microfinance offers a sustainable and responsive line of approach to issues of poverty alleviation and development, an approach which could avoid the excesses of capitalism on the one hand and the inefficiency of excessive state control on the other.

Some time ago, a very wealthy Indian couple from Mumbai came to see me. They asked for my blessings. I told them, as I tell so many others, that the only real blessings will come from themselves. To find blessings in their lives, I suggested, they should use their wealth to benefit the poor. After all, Mumbai has many slums where even basic necessities such as clean water are hard to come by. So, I told them, having made your money as capitalists, you should spend it as socialists!

In this connection I should mention that I am deeply impressed by philanthropists such as Bill and Melinda Gates and increasing numbers of others who share their resources with the global community on a massive scale. This is wonderful, and I appeal to others who have achieved a high degree of material success to become part of this noble trend.

New Challenges from Science

Recent years have seen rapid advances in fields such as genetics and biotechnology. In the fields of therapeutic and reproductive cloning, we are now gaining unprecedented power over the creation and manipulation of life itself. And the sequencing of the human genome, I am told, is also bringing about a revolution in medical science, shifting it from a biochemical to a genetically based model of therapy. Increasingly, scientists are able to do genetic forecasting, by which they can predict the likely course of a person's health. These advances raise many difficult choices, not only for doctors and parents, but also for employers and institutions. Some respond to the challenges presented by these new technologies with blanket condemnations—saying, for example, that all genetic modification is wrong—but I do not think these issues are so easy to dismiss. It is important that we meet our new areas of responsibility with sound motivation and critical discernment. I have discussed some of the issues related to new developments in biogenetics in an earlier book, *The Universe in a Single Atom.*

All the major challenges we face in the world call for an approach based on ethical awareness and inner values. Safeguarding the future is not just a matter of laws and government regulations; it also requires individual initiative. We need to change our way of thinking and to close the gap between perception and reality. For this reason, and in order to meet these challenges, education is crucial.

Educating Future Generations

When modern education began, religion was still an influential force in society, so the inculcation of virtues such as restraint, modesty, and service was part of family upbringing and participation in a religious community, and could therefore largely be taken for granted in an educational context. The main priority of modern universal education was therefore seen as imparting literary and technical knowledge. Today, however, the assumption that children will automatically be educated in ethics no longer seems realistic. Religion no longer has the influence it once had in society, and strong family values—which in the past were often grounded in religious faith and nurtured within strong community identities—have also been eroded, often by materialistic values and economic pressures. As a result, the inculcation of inner values in the young is no longer something we can take for granted. If we cannot assume that people learn spiritual and ethical values at home or through religious institutions, then it seems clear that the responsibility of schools in this area—spiritual and moral education—has greatly increased.

However, in an age of globalization and diverse societies, how we can meet this responsibility is no simple matter. If children in a given school, for example, come from diverse religious or cultural backgrounds, on what basis should the school conduct ethical education? To use a single religious perspective would be inadequate. In some parts of the world, religion is even excluded from the school curriculum. So how can schools give their pupils an ethical education which is unbiased and inclusive?

Whenever I speak at schools and universities about the need for greater attention to ethics and inner values, I get a very positive response. This suggests that educators and students too share my concern. What is required is a way of promoting inner values which is genuinely universal—which can embrace, without prejudice, both agnostic humanist perspectives and religious perspectives of various kinds.

In Canada in the autumn of 2009, I took part in an interesting dialogue on this subject and met many trainee teachers from all over the province of Quebec. Until quite recently Quebec had a rather traditional and predominantly Roman Catholic society. In recent decades, though, like many other parts of the world, it has become increasingly secular and, with immigration, has also become multicultural and multireligious. To reflect these changes, the provincial authorities are seeking new ways of teaching ethics in schools, ways that are less reliant on traditional religious approaches.

On specific questions—how to develop a syllabus, how to teach different age groups—I had little to offer, as these are matters for specialists in education, developmental psychology, and related fields. But on the general approach, I shared my view that in a secular approach to ethics it is crucial that the basic principles be genuinely universal.

I also shared my view that many people can benefit from formal exercises in attentiveness and the cultivation of inner values. It is with this in mind that I have elaborated some of these in the second part of this book.

On questions of pedagogy, my only suggestion was—and is—to remember that when teaching ethical awareness and inner values, providing information is never enough, and teaching by example is of paramount importance. If teachers talk about the value of kindness, elaborating its benefits, while failing to illustrate what they are saying through personal example, then students are unlikely to find their words compelling. If, on the other hand, teachers embody kindness in their own behavior by showing genuine concern for their students, they will make their point more effectively.

Of course, I do not mean to suggest that teachers should be too soft! On the contrary, the best teachers are often quite strict. But for strictness to be effective, it must be grounded in concern for the welfare of the students. Saying this reminds me of my late senior tutor, who was very dear to me. In outward appearance, Ling Rinpoché was quite stern. When I was studying as a young monk in Tibet, he kept two whips next to him during classes. One was an ordinary brown leather whip, reserved for use on my elder brother, and the other was a special yellow whip, reserved for me. In fact, the yellow whip was never used, but had it been, I'm sure it would have been no less painful than the one used one or twice on my unfortunate brother! Joking aside, teachers have tremendous influence on the development of children, not just in academic matters, but also as people. Different students have different needs, and teachers must be sensitive to this. Firm discipline may be good for some while a gentle approach is more suitable for others. In my own case, to this day I feel deep gratitude toward my tutors. Despite Ling Rinpoché's stern exterior, in time I came to appreciate the profundity of his kindness. In traditional Tibetan monastic education, there are many qualities admired in teachers, such as patience, enthusiasm, the ability to inspire, being energetic, and being good at presenting lessons clearly. But above all, three qualities are regarded as the marks of a great teacher: academic excellence (*khé*), moral integrity (*tsün*), and kindness (*sang*).

I am aware that teachers in modern societies often face tremendous challenges. Classes can be very large, the subjects taught can be very complex, and discipline can be difficult to maintain. Given the importance, and the difficulty, of teachers' jobs, I was surprised when I heard that in some western societies today teaching is regarded as a rather low-status profession. That is surely very muddled. Teachers must be applauded for choosing this career. They should congratulate themselves, particularly on days when they are exhausted and downhearted. They are engaged in work that will influence not just students' immediate level of knowledge but their entire lives, and thereby they have the potential to contribute to the future of humanity itself.

The Need for Perseverance

In the face of all the challenges of today's interconnected world, is my optimism about the future of humanity idealistic? Perhaps it is. Is it unrealistic? Certainly not. To remain indifferent to the challenges we face is indefensible. If the goal is noble, whether or not it is realized within our lifetimes is largely irrelevant. What we must do, therefore, is to strive and persevere and never give up.

Part II

EDUCATING THE HEART THROUGH TRAINING THE MIND

Introduction: Starting with Oneself

In the first half of this book, I offered an entirely secular basis on which to understand the importance of compassion and inner values. But understanding the need for these qualities is not enough. We must also act on this understanding. So how are we to bring this understanding and translate it into our everyday lives? How are we to become more compassionate, kinder, more forgiving, and more discerning in our behavior?

It is in response to such questions that, in the remaining chapters of this book, I offer some thoughts about ways in which we can begin to educate our hearts. Many aspects of these suggestions—about how to restrain our negative behavior; how to combat our destructive emotional tendencies; how to cultivate inner values such as compassion, patience, contentment, self-discipline, and generosity; and how to develop a calm and disciplined mind through mental training—are drawn from classical Buddhist traditions which are part of my own background, including especially that of "mind training," known as lojong *in Tibetan. In my view, however, the practices presented here require no religious belief or commitment. Instead they constitute an approach to living ethically and in harmony with others, with a deeper sense of well-being, which can be practiced in a way that is independent of any specific religious or cultural perspective.*

My suggestions in this second part are offered in the sincere hope that they can provide help and guidance for those who want to learn to overcome their own difficulties and to lead fulfilling ethical lives oriented toward the long-term benefit of both self and others.

Once again, I must emphasize that these suggestions are not an instant cure for all our problems. Educating the heart takes both time and sustained effort, though I have no doubt that with sincere motivation we can all learn kindheartedness, and we can all benefit from it.

8

Ethical Mindfulness in Everyday Life

ETHICS IS NOT simply a matter of knowing. More important, it is about doing. For this reason, even the most sophisticated ethical understanding, if it is not applied in daily life, is somewhat pointless. Living ethically requires not only the conscious adoption of an ethical outlook but also a commitment to developing and applying inner values in our daily lives.

Now, regarding the question of how to put ethics into practice in everyday life, it may be helpful to consider the process as having three aspects or levels—each progressively more advanced and dependent for its success upon the former. As outlined in some classical Buddhist texts, these are as follows: an ethic of restraint—deliberately refraining from doing actual or potential harm to others; an ethic of virtue—actively cultivating and enhancing our positive behavior and inner values; and an ethic of altruism—dedicating our lives, genuinely and selflessly, to the welfare of others.

To be effective, these three stages must be considered in relation to all our behavior. In other words, not just in relation to our outward physical actions, but also in relation to what we say, and ultimately to our very thoughts and intentions. And of these levels of behavior—body, speech, and mind—the most important is the mind, as the source of everything we do and say.

To concentrate our attention only on actions of body and speech would be like a doctor addressing only the symptoms of an illness rather than its underlying cause. For a treatment to be effective, it must also address the source of the problem. In view of this, the final three chapters are all primarily concerned with training the mind. But before moving on to the subject of educating the heart through training the mind, I should first say a few words about the importance of abandoning destructive habits of body and speech, as it is this which constitutes the first stage in the practice of ethics.

The Ethic of Restraint

Regarding certain kinds of obviously harmful behavior, all the world's major faiths and the humanistic traditions converge. Murder, theft, and inappropriate sexual conduct such as sexual exploitation are by definition harmful to others. So of course they should be abandoned.

But the ethic of restraint calls for more than this. Before we can contemplate actively benefiting others, we must first of all ensure that we do them no harm, even by our actions which are not immediately violent.

With regard to this principle of doing no harm, I am particularly impressed and humbled by my brothers and sisters in the Jain tradition. Jainism, which is something like a twin religion to

Buddhism, places great emphasis on the virtue of nonviolence, or *ahimsa,* toward all beings. For example, Jain monks go to great lengths to ensure that they do not accidentally tread on insects or harm other living beings in their everyday activities.

However, the exemplary behavior of Jain monks and nuns is hard for all of us to emulate. Even for those whose circle of primary concern is restricted to humanity rather than encompassing all sentient beings, it can be very hard not to contribute to harming others through our actions in indirect ways. Consider, for example, how rivers come to be polluted: perhaps by mining companies extracting minerals, or industrial plants producing components that are crucial to the technologies we use on a daily basis. Every user of those technologies thereby is partly responsible for the pollution and thus contributes negatively to the lives of others. Unfortunately, it is perfectly possible to harm others indirectly through our actions without any intention of doing so.

So, realistically, I think the most important thing we can all do to minimize the harm we inflict in our everyday lives is to apply discernment in our behavior, and to follow that natural sense of conscientiousness which arises from the enhanced awareness that discernment brings us.

Harm Caused by Nonviolent Means

While harm inflicted by outward actions can normally be seen, the suffering we inflict on others with words can be more hidden but is often no less damaging. This is particularly the case in our closest, most intimate relationships. We humans are quite sensitive, and it is easy to inflict suffering on those around us through our careless use of harsh words.

We can also inflict harm with dishonesty, slander, and divisive gossip. No doubt we have all, at some time or another, felt the negative consequences of such idle talk. It undermines trust and affection and can create all kinds of unfortunate misunderstandings and enmities between people. Here, as in other areas, we need to observe the "golden rule" found in all of the world's ethical systems: "Treat others as you would wish to be treated yourself" or "Do unto others as you would have them do unto you."

When it comes to avoiding harmful actions of body and speech, in addition to this fundamental rule, I personally find a list of six principles from a text by the second-century Indian thinker Nagarjuna to be helpful. In this text, Nagarjuna is offering advice to an Indian monarch of the time. The six principles are as follows:

Avoid excessive use of intoxicants.
Uphold the principle of right livelihood.
Ensure that one's body, speech, and mind are nonviolent.
Treat others with respect.
Honor those worthy of esteem, such as parents, teachers, and those who are kind.
Be kind to others.

In spelling out what constitutes "right livelihood," Nagarjuna lists the following examples of a wrong approach to livelihood: trying to gain material benefits from others through pretense; using attractive words to gain things from others through deceit; praising another's possessions with the intention of trying to obtain them for oneself; forcibly taking what belongs to someone else; and extolling the qualities of what one has obtained in the past with the hope of receiving more.

Most of these pertain, in one form or another, to being dishonest. Dishonesty destroys the foundations of others' trust and is profoundly harmful. Transparency in our dealings with others is therefore tremendously important. Many of the scandals we hear about today, notably the corruption which is observable at so many levels and in so many fields—government, the judiciary, international finance, politics, media, even international sports—are related to this issue of right livelihood.

Heedfulness, Mindfulness, and Awareness

Just as a carpenter would not think of mending a chair without having a chisel, hammer, and saw near at hand, so too do we require a basic toolkit to help us in our daily effort to live ethically. In Buddhist tradition this toolkit is described in terms of three interrelated factors known as *heedfulness, mindfulness,* and *introspective awareness.* These three ideas may also be useful in a secular context. Together they can help us retain our core values in everyday life and guide our day-to-day behavior so that it becomes more in tune with the aim of bringing benefit to self and others.

The first of these, heedfulness, refers to adopting an overall stance of caution. The Tibetan term *bhakyö,* often translated as "heedfulness" or "conscientiousness," carries the sense of being careful and attentive. For example, if we are diagnosed as having diabetes, the doctor will advise us to be very careful with our diet. We must avoid sugar, salt, and fatty foods to keep our blood pressure and insulin in check. The doctor will warn us that if we fail to adhere to this dietary regime there may be serious consequences for our health. When patients care about their health, they will follow this advice and adopt an attitude of caution regarding their diet. When they are tempted to eat something they should avoid, this attitude or stance of caution will help them exercise restraint.

In one classical Buddhist text, heedfulness is illustrated with a story about a man convicted of a crime who is ordered by the king to carry a bowl of sesame oil, full to the brim, while a guard walks next to him carrying an unsheathed sword. The convict is warned that if he so much as spills a single drop of oil, he will be struck down with the sword. We can imagine how careful and vigilant the convict would be! He would have complete presence of mind and total attentiveness. The story illustrates how closely related heedfulness is to the qualities of mindfulness and awareness described below.

Today there are many secularized techniques for the development of mindfulness, and these have been shown to be effective in stress reduction and the treatment of depression. As I understand it, mindfulness in this context usually refers to gaining awareness of our own patterns of behavior, including thoughts and feelings, and learning to let go of those habits, thoughts, and emotions which are unhelpful. This seems a very worthwhile endeavor. How we might go about further developing this kind of awareness is a subject to which I will return in Chapter 9.

Yet, in the context of living ethically on a day-to-day basis, in my view the most important meaning of mindfulness is *recollection.* In other words, mindfulness is the ability to gather oneself mentally and thereby recall one's core values and motivation. In Tibetan the word for mindfulness, *drenpa,* also means "memory," so it suggests bringing presence of mind into everyday activities. With such recollection, we are less likely to indulge our bad habits and more likely to refrain from harmful deeds. Littering, being wasteful, and overindulging oneself are all simple examples of behavior which can be improved through the application of mindfulness.

Awareness, or *sheshin* in Tibetan, means paying attention to our own behavior. It means honestly observing our behavior as it is going on, and thereby bringing it under control. By being aware of our words and actions, we guard ourselves against doing and saying things we will later regret. When we are angry, for instance, and if we fail to recognize that our anger is distorting our perception, we may say things we do not mean. So having the ability to monitor oneself, having, as it were, a second-order level of attention, is of great practical use in everyday life, as it gives us greater control over our negative behavior and enables us to remain true to our deeper motives and convictions.

Such awareness of our own behavior—our actions, thoughts, and words—is not something we can learn overnight. Rather, it develops gradually, and as we become more aware, we slowly gain mastery.

To some readers, this mental toolkit may sound very like the advice to "listen to your conscience," an idea which plays an important role in many religious approaches to the practice of ethics. And indeed there are many similarities between the two. In some religions, conscience is regarded as a precious gift from God which makes human beings uniquely moral creatures. From a secular perspective, we may understand conscience as a product of our biological nature as social animals, or as something we acquire from society through our upbringing and environment. Either way, all sane and responsible people will surely agree that this quality is of great significance with respect to our moral sensibility. Whatever one's views about religion, the idea of a person devoid of conscience—without any inner voice of restraint or moral responsibility—is truly frightening.

Practicing awareness is not quite the same as listening to your conscience, however. In Buddhist ethical theory there is no idea of the conscience as a distinct mental faculty. But being conscientious is still very important. It is described in terms of two key mental qualities, namely *self-respect* and *consideration of others.*

The first of these, self-respect, relates to having a sense of personal integrity, a self-image as a person who upholds certain values. So when we are tempted to indulge in harmful behavior, our self-image acts as a restraint, as we think "this is unbecoming of me." The second mental quality, consideration of others, pertains to having a healthy regard for others' opinions, especially for their potential disapproval. Together, these two factors give us an added level of caution about doing wrong which can strengthen our moral compass.

The Ethic of Virtue

If, through mindfulness, awareness, and heedfulness, we can manage to refrain from harming others in our everyday actions and words, we can start to give more serious attention to actively doing good, and this can be a source of great joy and inner confidence. We can benefit others through our actions by being warm and generous toward them, by being charitable, and by helping those in need. Therefore, when misfortune befalls others, or they make mistakes, rather than responding with ridicule or blame, we must reach out and help them. Benefiting others through our speech includes praising others, listening to their problems, and offering them advice and encouragement.

To help us bring benefit to others through our words and actions, it is useful to cultivate an attitude of sympathetic joy in others' achievements and good fortune. This attitude is a powerful antidote against envy, which is not only a source of unnecessary suffering on the individual level but also an obstacle to our ability to reach out and engage with others. Tibetan teachers often say that such sympathetic joy is the least costly way of promoting one's own virtues.

The Ethic of Altruism

Altruism is a genuinely selfless dedication of one's actions and words to the benefit of others. All the world's religious traditions recognize this as the highest form of ethical practice, and in many it is seen as the main avenue to liberation or to unity with God.

But though a complete and selfless dedication to others is the highest form of ethical practice, this does not mean that altruism cannot be undertaken by anyone. In fact many people in caring professions such as social work and health care, and also those in teaching, are involved in the pursuit of this third level of ethics. Such professions, which bring direct benefit to the lives of so many, are truly noble. Yet there are countless other ways in which ordinary people can and do lead lives which benefit others. What is required is simply that we make serving others a priority.

An important part of serving others is using discernment to assess the likely consequences of our own actions. Then, by being heedful, mindful, and attentive in our everyday lives, we will begin to gain mastery over our actions and words. This is the very foundation of freedom, and it is through gaining such self-mastery, and using it to ensure that our actions are non-harmful at every level, that we can start to actively work for the benefit of others.

9

Dealing with Destructive Emotions

IF, AS I HAVE suggested, the key to human happiness lies in our own state of mind, so too do the primary obstacles to that happiness. Without a doubt the greatest impediments to our individual well-being and our ability to live a spiritually fulfilling life are our own persistent propensities toward destructive or afflictive emotions. Such emotions are the real enemies of human happiness and the ultimate source of all destructive human behavior. Tackling these negative emotions is an important goal of ethical and spiritual practice.

But before offering some practical suggestions as to how we might go about dealing with these destructive tendencies and reducing their grip on our daily habits and behavior, I must first address the question of whether this a realistic goal. Do we human beings actually have the ability to change ourselves from within?

The Possibility of Self-Improvement

The world religions have long recognized that we humans have the capacity to change from within. But in a purely secular context, demonstrating the reality of this capacity can be challenging. A committed materialist, for instance, may argue that we are completely determined by biology, or, to use a contemporary phrase, that we are "hard-wired" in certain ways. In such a view, some people are determined by nature to be angry, while others are naturally more inclined toward kindness; some are genetically disposed to be optimistic, while others have an innate propensity for depression. Given that many of our character traits do indeed seem to be inherited, and that afflictive emotions like anger, hatred, and jealousy are part of our nature, it may also be right that there is nothing we can do about them. So, we may feel, perhaps it really is impossible to change the mental disposition we are born with.

If there really were nothing we could do about our emotions, we would truly be slaves to them. However, evidence is gradually emerging from science, especially psychology and neuroscience, to suggest that it is possible to achieve meaningful change in our emotional and behavioral patterns through conscious effort. Of course, as I have said before, I myself am no scientist. Nevertheless, for many years I have been discussing these issues with experts. From these conversations, it seems that the recent discovery of what is called "brain plasticity" may well offer a scientific explanation for this possibility of meaningful change. Researchers have observed that the patterns and structures of the brain can and do change over time in response to our thoughts and experiences. Moreover, scientists are now able to observe the interaction between those parts of the brain associated with higher cognitive activities such as rational thought (in the prefrontal cortex) and those parts known as the limbic system, including the almond-shaped amygdala, which are associated with our most primitive instinctual and emotional reflexes. These advances in neuroscience have prompted many scientists to give serious attention to the idea that, through our own conscious efforts, we may be able to train our emotional instincts by literally altering the physical patterns in our brain. Research in this area is still quite new, but it seems to me that it may potentially provide the committed materialist with grounds for hope as strong as the faith of the religious believer.

The World of Our Emotions

Interestingly, in the classical Buddhist science of mind in which I am trained, there is no concept of emotion as a single category that precisely corresponds to the understanding of emotion in contemporary western psychology. Indeed, there is no word in either Sanskrit or classical Tibetan that exactly translates the word "emotion." Instead, all mental states are understood to include both cognitive and feeling dimensions to some degree, and to contain five omnipresent mental factors, of which "feeling" is one. The other four are discrimination, volition, attention, and contact. So even a cognitive mental process as simple as counting from one to ten is regarded as having some kind of "feeling" or "feeling tone," which naturally is related to context.

There are also various ways of categorizing our emotional states. For example, in contemporary psychology the main distinction is often drawn between emotional states which, on the one hand, are pleasurable or joyful and are described as positive, and those which, on the other hand, are unpleasant or painful and are described as negative.

In classical Buddhist psychology, however, the distinction is rather different. Instead, the primary distinction is not between those states which are pleasurable and those that are painful, but between those that are beneficial and those that are harmful. "Afflictive" mental states, known as *nyonmong* in Tibetan or *klesha* in Sanskrit, are those which undermine our long-term well-being, while "non-afflictive" mental states are those which have no such destructive impact.

Given these different ways of categorizing emotional experience, it is important for readers not to confuse those emotions which are afflictive—that is to say, harmful to our long-term well-being—with those which simply don't feel good. Of course, sometimes these overlap. Feelings of hatred, for example, are both destructive and unpleasant to experience, but there can also be experiences which may not be pleasant but can nevertheless be beneficial, and in the same way there can be feelings that are pleasant which nevertheless can be destructive. For instance, feelings of sadness, grief, and remorse are certainly not pleasurable, but they need not in themselves be afflictive. When faced, say, with the death of a loved one, feelings of grief and sorrow may actually be quite constructive in helping us come to terms with our loss and and move on with our lives. In the same way, emotions which may initially seem pleasurable can nevertheless be destructive at a deeper level by undermining our mental peace and stability. One example might be lust, or excessive longing for a particular object. Such longing may in some sense seem pleasurable. But eventually obsessive craving will erode our capacity for genuine contentment and undermine our mental equilibrium, and should therefore be considered destructive.

In the context of secular ethics, this distinction between those mental states which undermine well-being—our own and that of others—and those which promote survival and well-being can be very useful, since it is directly relevant to our pursuit of happiness and an ethically sound way of life. Given that people come from many different backgrounds and cultures, which states are to be considered destructive and which are to be considered beneficial may vary in particular cases. Generally speaking, we can define destructive emotions as those states which undermine our well-being by creating inner turmoil, thereby undermining self-control and depriving us of mental freedom. Within this, it is also possible to distinguish between two subcategories: those emotional states that are destructive in themselves, such as greed, hatred, or malice; and those states, such as attachment, anger, or fear, which only become destructive when their intensity is disproportionate to the situation in which they arise.

From a biological perspective, all our basic emotions evidently have evolutionary purposes. For example, attachment helps bring us together and enables us to create bonds, anger helps us repel forces that are detrimental to our survival and well-being, fear enables us to respond to a threat with vigilance, and envy prompts us to compete with others so that we do not overlook our own needs. Scientists have demonstrated that these basic emotions have clear biological dimensions. When we face an immediate danger, for example, and fear arises, extra blood rushes to our legs, and with increased adrenaline and our hearts beating faster, the emotion of fear literally prepares us to flee. In contrast, when anger arises, more blood goes to our arms, preparing us to confront the threat. So the important point to bear in mind is that these feelings are not destructive in themselves; they become destructive only when their intensity is out of proportion to the situation, or when they arise in situations that do not call for them.

As for attachment, which after all is the feeling that holds families and communities together, we do not usually think of it as destructive. However, when this basic emotion becomes excessive and wants to control its object, it does become destructive. This is true also of desire. In itself, desire is not destructive. After all, without desire, the human race would cease to exist altogether! In fact, desire is the emotion that drives many of our day-to-day activities—from getting up in the morning to eating, working, and pursuing our immediate and long-term goals in life.

Similarly, even anger is not always destructive. For example, in some situations strong compassion may give rise to an equally strong sense of outrage—that is, anger—about an injustice. Again, feeling angry can, in the short term, make our minds more focused and give us an extra burst of energy and determination. In these ways, anger can, in certain situations, make us more effective in getting things done and in obtaining what we rightly seek. However, when anger extends beyond this practical function, most of the energy it brings us is not helpful at all. Since all of us have probably, at one time or another, been on the receiving end of other people's anger, we all have experience of its unpleasant consequences.

However, while anger may sometimes have a constructive element, hatred never does. Hatred is always destructive.

Like anger, fear is not destructive in every situation. Fear makes us more attentive and guards us against danger. It is also a powerful motivating factor, forcing us to be cautious and to take care of our well-being. But when fear is obsessive, it can paralyze us and become a very destructive mental condition. Furthermore, excessive fear gives rise to a persistent state of anxiety, which is harmful to our health. I therefore often distinguish between reasonable fear and unreasonable fear. The first kind is not only legitimate but actually necessary to our survival. If a mad dog comes running at us, we need to respond to this danger with fear. This is obvious. In contrast, unreasonable fear occurs when the source of threat is largely our own mental projection. We need to keep this kind of fear in check, for it is totally useless and often destructive. What we need to counter unreasonable fear is a better understanding of the situation at hand.

This dual aspect of emotions—that all of them have destructive and nondestructive sides—can also be seen in other mental states such as doubt, shame, grief, competitiveness, and even our sense of ego itself. Doubt is the mental factor that enables us to inquire and seek out understanding. Indeed, I always say that a dose of skepticism is quite healthy in that it opens our minds to questioning and new knowledge. However, when doubt becomes pathological it can paralyze us and prevent us from taking any decisive action. The same is true of shame. At the basic level, shame is an important social emotion which has a constructive function; nevertheless, when shame becomes extreme, it can lead to low self-regard and negative self-judgment, which are clearly not constructive. With respect to grief or sorrow, in some situations this emotion is constructive and has a positive effect. But when it becomes something like a habit of mind, divorced from any realistic cause, it may be destructive, as when it manifests as self-absorbed grief or as depression.

Competitiveness, too, can be constructive, as when our competitive urge motivates us to strive to achieve something better or higher. However, when competitiveness acquires an aspect of wanting to put others down or hold them back so we can outachieve them, it then becomes destructive.

In egoism, too, we can distinguish between two kinds. A strong sense of self can be constructive, the basis for generating self-confidence—the state of mind that allows us to feel, "Yes, I can do this." But another form of egoism is evident when, in pursuing our own self-interest, we become totally oblivious to others' welfare and even willing to exploit others to benefit ourselves. This type of egoism is clearly destructive.

So, when we are dealing with matters as subtle as human mental processes, it is important not to be too dogmatic. It is difficult or impossible to determine whether or not a given mental state is destructive without knowing its context. Often we can make this determination only by taking into account the underlying motivation, the specific object of the emotion, the consequences of the emotion, and so on. In the area of the human mind, therefore, we should always maintain an attitude of open-mindedness, pragmatism, and flexibility.

Shared Features of Destructive Emotions

One feature that characterizes all destructive emotions is a tendency to distort our perception of reality. They cause us to narrow our perspective so that we fail to see a given situation in its wider context. For example, when we are feeling an extreme form of attachment—such as intense desire, lust, or greed—often we are projecting a level of attractiveness onto the object of our desire which far exceeds what is really there. We become blind even to quite obvious shortcomings, and in our obsessive clinging we create a kind of insecurity in ourselves, a feeling that we *need* to obtain the object of our desire and are incomplete without it. Excessive attachment tends also to involve a desire to control, which can be very suffocating when the object of that desire happens to be another person. Because of this, extreme attachment is by nature quite unstable. One moment we may feel great affection for something or someone, but when, for example, our desire for control is thwarted, this feeling can easily turn to resentment or hatred.

A similar loss of perspective characterizes extreme or intense emotions of aversion, such as anger, hatred, contempt, or resentment. When we are gripped by intense anger, for example, the object of our rage will always appear one hundred percent negative, even though in moments of calm we may recognize that the same person or thing has many admirable qualities. The overly strong emotion causes us to lose our capacity for discernment. We cannot see the long- and short-term consequences of our actions, and as a result we are unable to distinguish between right and wrong. We literally, for a moment, become almost mad, incapable of acting in our own best interest. And then, after the event, when the emotion cools, how often we regret what we have done or said in anger!

On a trip to Sweden some years ago, I had a lengthy conversation with Dr. Aaron Beck, one of the founding fathers of cognitive behavior therapy, a major branch of modern psychotherapy which has been quite effective in treating behavioral problems and depression. When we met, Dr. Beck was in his early eighties. It was very interesting to me how close many of his observations were to the insights of classical Buddhist psychology. For example, he said that in intense anger, almost ninety percent of the quality of repulsiveness we see in the object of our anger is an exaggeration and a projection. This is in close accord with the understanding found in classical Buddhist texts.

The point about all these afflictive mental states is that, in one way or another, they obscure our vision by clouding our capacity for discernment. They make us incapable of rational judgment, and thus we might say they steal our minds.

The Emotion Families

One helpful approach to understanding our destructive emotions is to view them as related families distinguished by the kind of underlying state of mind they involve. For example, as I have said, the emotions of the anger family, such as hatred, enmity, and malice, are characterized by an exaggerated repulsion, while those of the attachment family, such as greed, lust, and craving, are characterized by an equally exaggerated sense of attraction. The other main families of afflictive emotions—envy, pride, and doubt—involve mixtures of excessive attraction on the one hand (such as the excessive attachment to a deluded self-image in the case of pride) and excessive repulsion on the other (such as the excessive sense of enmity toward a rival in the case of envy). As we have already seen, in addition to this element of excessive revulsion or attraction or unhealthy mixtures of the two, all afflictive emotions are further characterized by an unrealistic or deluded perspective.

Envy is a somewhat complex family of afflictions, since its root lies in attachment and attraction yet it also has a strong element of anger, hostility, and repulsion. Recent scientific research on happiness has found that one of the primary sources of discontent in today's world, especially in the more affluent societies, is our human tendency to compare ourselves to those around us. Fundamentally this comes down to the problem of envy.

The afflictive family of pride or conceit, which includes destructive attitudes such as arrogance, prejudice, and even obsessive or unrealistic embarrassment, also involves a mixture of attraction and repulsion: attraction, for example, to an unrealistic or deluded self-image, and repulsion or disdain toward anyone or anything that threatens that cherished self-image. This attachment to an inflated self-image, whether based on social status, accomplishment, or the circumstances of our birth, may prompt us to actions that are disrespectful of others, and such actions are destructive both to the welfare of others and to ourselves.

Finally, there is the family of afflictive doubt, which encompasses such destructive emotions as anxiety and obsessive guilt. These are grounded in habitual fear and in unrealistic self-loathing, which are very damaging to our ability to be compassionate. Emotions of the afflictive doubt family can therefore be highly detrimental to our own sense of well-being.

These then are the destructive emotions which I consider the main obstacles to human well-being—not only our own individual well-being, but also that of those around us, and ultimately that of the very world we share. These emotions fundamentally undermine our capacity to put positive ethical values, such as compassion, into practice. Only when we fully recognize the negative repercussions of such destructive emotions and expose their futility and impracticality as responses will we be able to go about tackling them effectively.

Our inner development with regard to regulating our destructive emotions calls for a two-pronged approach. On the one hand, we must seek to reduce the impact of the destructive potentials that are inherent within us; on the other, we must seek to enhance the positive qualities that also naturally exist within us. This two-pronged approach to mental training is what I consider to be the heart of genuine spiritual practice.

Taking a Stance

In order to go about dealing with these destructive emotions, it is first of all necessary to adopt a general attitude or stance toward them: a stance of opposition.

Such a stance involves recognizing that the law of opposition—whereby positives cancel out or neutralize negatives—applies not just to the physical world but also to our inner or mental world. In the great wisdom traditions we find clear lessons both on the mental states that are to be tackled and on the need to cultivate and deploy their antidotes. If no opposing forces exist for our destructive emotions, then there is nothing we can do about them. However, if opposite, positive forces do exist, then they can become powerful antidotes. For example, the main antidote for anger is forbearance, for greed is contentment, for fear is courage, and for doubt is understanding.

A key element in generating an effective stance of opposition toward negative emotions is a deep recognition of their destructive nature and a conviction that we both can and should strive to overcome them. This conviction can then serve as the basis for an enduring resolve to tackle them. We can develop this element of the general stance by giving attentive, compassionate consideration to the destructive effects these emotions have upon the lives of ourselves and those around us. We can reflect on the fact that such emotions—hatred and greed, for example—not only are the sources of many of our personal problems, but also are the ultimate sources of many of our collective problems, such as war, poverty, and environmental degradation. Simply adopting a stance of opposition toward our destructive emotions will have an immediate influence by giving us a sense of caution, which is a critical defense when such powerful emotions strike us. So it is very important to give careful consideration to the negative impact of each of our most persistent destructive tendencies.

If our mind is lost, even for a short time, to an emotion as destructive as hatred, we may say and do terrible things. The damage created by one moment of intense hatred can be devastating. In Buddhism, the human mind is often compared to a wild elephant. As some farmers know well, when an elephant is agitated, it can wreak great destruction. But an unruly, agitated human mind, given to fits of rage, malice, obsessive craving, jealousy, or arrogance, can wreak even more destruction than a rampaging elephant, and can ruin lives.

To counter these tremendously powerful destructive emotions we all have within us, we need to develop very strong enthusiasm and determination for the task. This enthusiasm will come, in large part, from considering the negative impact of those emotions. In addition to being powerfully destructive in moments of intense feeling, they can also have an insidious, corrosive effect on our inner well-being. Gradually and surely they undermine our inner peace, deprive us of mental freedom, and hinder the expression of our empathetic nature, the source of our greatest happiness. In fact, we could even say that all the violence and destruction in the world are the result of hatred. The damaging consequences of hatred can be observed at individual, family, and global levels.

So I encourage people to contemplate the destructive nature of such emotions on a regular basis. This is a subject to which I return in Chapter 11, where I describe some simple mental training practices which can be helpful as a means to developing conviction about the need to overcome such emotions, and as a means to training the mind.

Understanding the Causes of Affliction

Having developed a strong resolve to tackle our destructive emotions, we can then reflect upon their causes. Where do these disturbing emotions come from? Well, we may respond, they come from the world we live in, and from others who do us wrong! If it weren't for other people, we may think, we would have no reason to feel aggressive, resentful, or anxious.

This response—seeing the source of our problems in external conditions—is a natural one, especially when we are not used to paying attention to our internal mental processes. We tend to see the troublemaker as something outside ourselves. If we reflect deeply, however, we discover that the real troublemaker is within us; our true enemies are our own destructive tendencies. For if the external condition is the real source of our trouble, it follows that if, say, ten people are confronted with the same external situation, each of them should encounter the same difficulty when faced with that external condition. This we know is not the case. The way we react emotionally to any given situation depends to a large extent on our own outlook, our own attitude, and our own emotional habits.

As part of learning to gain a measure of control over our emotions as a step toward developing a calm mind, it is important that we take a measured and, above all, realistic approach to dealing with the world and the problems we face. Take anger, for example. Is getting angry really a helpful response? If we have a hostile neighbor who constantly provokes us, does getting angry do anything to remedy the situation? What is more, if we allow anger and resentment to fester, they will gradually wear us down, affecting our moods, our sleep, even our appetite. And if this happens, our hostile neighbor really will have won some kind of victory! This is the way of a foolish person, for it is a kind of self-torture. If, in contrast, we can sustain some tranquility of mind, maintain our composure, and carry on with our normal lives, then we will be much better equipped to determine the most effective course of action for dealing with such situations. The truth is that when we are agitated we are not much good at anything—even hitting a nail straight can be problematic!

Upon reflection, then, we start to see that it is a mistake to understand the causes of our disturbing emotions purely in terms of the things, or the people, who trigger them in us. If we step back and take some time to reflect, we find that even though our grievances may to some extent be legitimate, our feelings of irritation and frustration are actually rather unrealistic and often exaggerated beyond what the actual situation merits. We may also find that such disturbing emotions recur over and over, not just because of external factors, but also because they have become something of an emotional habit for us.

When we start to see things from this perspective, we can begin to recognize that these destructive emotions feed on themselves—that the more they are indulged, the stronger they become. To realistically address such self-perpetuating destructive emotions, therefore, requires us to turn our attention to our own habits of mind. Instead of looking to blame others and the world around us, we should first look within ourselves.

This is a point the eighth-century Buddhist thinker Shantideva makes very well when discussing the problem of anger. If we wish to prevent our feet from being pricked by thorns, he says, it would be foolish to attempt to cover the whole world in leather. Much easier, and more effective, is to cover the soles of our own feet. In the same way, it is a mistake to think we will get rid of anger by changing everything in the world that makes us angry. Instead, we should look to change ourselves.

What anger most depends on for its perpetuation is our own inner dissatisfaction, the state of latent irritation or lack of contentment which in Tibetan we call *yi mi-dewa*. It is this general underlying mental unease which makes us susceptible to the triggering of destructive emotions, especially anger. Such inner dissatisfaction is the fuel upon which destructive emotions such as anger and hostility depend. Therefore, just as extinguishing the initial sparks is a more effective method of preventing fire damage than waiting until the fire is blazing, in the same manner, dealing with the underlying causes of discontent is a more effective way to prevent destructive emotions from doing damage than waiting until the emotions become full blown.

Emotional Awareness

If we are to succeed in effectively tackling our destructive tendencies, first of all, we must observe and study them closely. For dealing with destructive propensities is not merely a matter of suppressing them. Our emotional and psychological habits can be very deep-seated, and often have developed over the course of many years. So if we do not address such emotions honestly but bottle them up, this can potentially have very counterproductive effects. In fact, ignoring or suppressing emotions can actually aggravate them and make them intensify until they surge to the surface and, like a swollen river bursting its banks, find expression in unexpected negative thoughts and behavior. Instead of suppressing our destructive emotions, therefore, we must be open and honest with ourselves and bring mindful awareness to what triggers them, how they make us feel, and what kind of behavior they provoke. This kind of introspective attentiveness to the way these emotions arise within us and manifest in our behavior is what I call emotional awareness. It is only by practicing such awareness—by facing these emotions directly and giving them careful scrutiny—that we can gradually bring them under control.

Here again, it is worth considering our behavior in terms of the three dimensions—at the levels of body, speech, and most important, mind. If we can maintain introspective attentiveness to these three aspects of our experience and behavior, then we can, by stages, develop an emotional awareness which will be very helpful in restraining our negative impulses.

Attentiveness

Attentiveness to emotional experience is very beneficial, but at first, it is surprisingly difficult to achieve. In fact, trying to identify emotions at the moment they arise may initially seem impossible. In large part this is because they are simply so swift, and in that split second when powerful emotion arises in us, it seems to occupy all of our consciousness. As a result, the process by which they unfold remains opaque to us. Such difficulties are natural, and should not make us feel dejected or discouraged. Instead we should remember that emotional awareness will only develop gradually, with patient perseverance. For this reason, we cannot begin by tackling our emotions directly, but have to start by focusing on their outward manifestations in our behavior.

In this context, it is helpful to consider the onset of destructive emotion as a kind of causal chain, which starts with an external stimulus and ends with our behavioral response. The aim of emotional awareness is to bring our attention or mindfulness into this split-second process, and thereby to gain some control over it.

Imagine, for example, that a door slams. Next comes our physical perception of that stimulus through the faculties of hearing, sight, and perhaps touch. Initially, this is a purely physical event, not yet colored by any interpretation. But then, less than a millisecond later, comes the interpretation. Here an element of projection or exaggeration is often involved: the split-second judgment that so-and-so deliberately slammed the door as an insult, for example. Interpretation is very quickly followed by the emotional response, perhaps anger, annoyance, or irritation. Then finally, also often very quickly, comes our behavioral response: we say something, or do something, in retaliation.

Once we understand this causal chain, the aim is to interrupt its flow by, as it were, "catching ourselves" and bringing awareness into the process. Generally speaking, it is easiest to start near the end—between the emotional reaction and its behavioral expression. Then, as we become more familiar with the process and our emotional awareness develops over time, we can work our way back along the causal chain, with the ultimate goal of quelling or eliminating the afflictive emotion altogether.

Catching Oneself

Thus our initial efforts should be directed toward ensuring that our destructive emotional responses do not translate into physical or verbal action. The idea is to catch ourselves before we start exploding, and to exercise restraint. This reminds me of a well-known Tibetan story about Ben Gungyal, a former robber turned spiritual teacher. One day while Ben Gungyal was visiting someone's house, his host left him alone. Since he was so habituated to stealing, his right hand instinctively reached out to take something. At that very instant he caught himself, literally grabbing his right arm with his left, and screamed, "There is a thief! There is a thief here!"

To help us learn to catch ourselves, it is useful to become familiar with the ways in which our destructive emotional experiences affect us physically. For example, what does it feel like when you first become annoyed? Does your heartbeat change? Do you feel any tightening in the face? Is there any tension in your arms or shoulders? Or what do you feel when you first encounter a sight that disgusts you? Is there any tensing of muscles? Then again, what sensations accompany feelings of jealousy or envy? Perhaps you feel these in your stomach, or in your chest?

As well as learning to recognize the physical manifestations of our emotions, we can try to observe our physical and mental responses to these sensations. Do we act in a certain way, say certain things, have certain thoughts? Do we clutch at our foreheads, or clench our fists? Perhaps we feel an urge to walk or to stand, or maybe just to fidget? Does our voice change when we become agitated? Perhaps the sound becomes louder or shriller? Do words come quicker to the mind? If we are working or talking when such an emotion arises, how does the emotion affect our work or the content of what we are saying?

Paying attention to such details helps us familiarize ourselves with our emotional states, and with greater familiarity we gain greater control. Often the simple acts of detaching ourselves from these emotional states and examining them help them subside.

Once you become quite familiar with this process and begin to have a measure of success in restraining your behavioral responses, you can then move one step back along the causal chain and try to prevent the emotion itself from reaching an explosive stage. In other words, you can learn to calm yourself the moment you become aware of the onset of strong emotion. Doing this may involve, for example, taking several deep breaths, or it may involve simply diverting your mind from the source of irritation. Or you may be able to view a given situation in a more positive light, as in the example of the Palestinian youth who learned to see the image of God in the faces of the soldiers at Israeli checkpoints. Sometimes, even if the actual situation is tragic, looking at it in the context of its multiple causes and conditions can help defuse strong negative emotional reactions. It is also helpful to view the situation from different angles or perspectives, so that what looks like a tragedy from one angle can also be seen to have positive by-products.

As you become more and more familiar with this approach, you will gradually gain greater mastery, to the point at which you may be able to catch yourself before the emotion even arises. By becoming aware of how feelings such as anger, irritation, or annoyance usually arise in you, you can learn to recognize what triggers them and can therefore arm yourself against them by bringing awareness to bear earlier in the process. Eventually, through practice, you can desensitize yourself to the triggers themselves, by not allowing an element of projection to distort your interpretation of events. This final stage can be very difficult, but if you can achieve it, it will also be tremendously liberating. For even when you encounter the stimulus—hostile words from another person, for instance—your awareness will guard you against instinctive interpretations which are clouded by exaggeration and projection, thereby enabling you to respond calmly and with discernment.

The Question of Moods

In the United States in recent years, I have enjoyed a number of dialogues with Dr. Paul Ekman, one of the pioneers of the scientific study of emotion, or what is called "affective neuroscience." In Dr. Ekman's view, it is not our emotions, which he describes as fleeting, that are the most harmful to our well-being, but our *moods.* While emotions come and go quite quickly, moods are more enduring, and because they are largely latent, underlying our state of mind but without any particular focus, they can also be somewhat hidden to our conscious awareness and therefore harder to tackle. It is moods, Dr. Ekman says, which make us more susceptible to certain emotions, and it is to them that we should turn our attention. This, I think, is a helpful observation.

In my understanding, emotions, moods, and personal traits can all be treated as kindred phenomena, which lie along a kind of a continuum, each having a more enduring quality than the former. For this reason, the fundamental ways of dealing with them are largely the same. However, the question of moods also raises the issue of a person's general level of energy, both physical and mental. In Buddhist tradition there is a strong emphasis, particularly in the context of mental training, on countering the opposing problems of excessive laxity, dullness, or sloth on the one hand and excessive excitement on the other. I think these kinds of advice, which I discuss further in Chapter 11, may have some bearing on the issue of tackling our moods. Also, while moods may appear to be very difficult to dislodge, I think we all have experienced a mood lifting very quickly in response to some good news. This shows that they are not as stable and enduring as they may seem. Sometimes a mood can be the product of some emotion bottled up inside, and when you release that emotion by talking with someone, perhaps apologizing for something you regret or even sharing a joke, your mood can quickly change. Of course, such relief can be temporary, somewhat like the relief you get from taking painkillers. So, in the end, the most effective way to deal with moods is to deal with the underlying emotions themselves.

There is no doubt that dealing with our negative propensities is very challenging. Faced with life's daily setbacks, we can all too easily fall into old negative habits of mind such as frustration, anger, or despondency. What we need, therefore, is a constant renewal of our effort to live by the values we want to uphold.

10

Cultivating Key Inner Values

LET US RECALL the two-pronged approach to genuine ethical practice: on the one hand, working to restrain our destructive emotions; on the other, actively cultivating our positive inner qualities. In the previous chapter I discussed the problem of destructive emotions and explored ways in which, through awareness and regulation of them, we can deal constructively with the challenges they pose. In this chapter I consider the other arm of this approach. Of the positive qualities that naturally exist within us, the most important, compassion, I have already spoken of at some length. I have also said something about the virtue of forgiveness in the context of justice. What follows here is a brief consideration of a few of the other key human values: patience or forbearance, contentment, self-discipline, and generosity.

Patience and Forbearance

In the context of secular ethics, perhaps the antidote to destructive emotion with the most urgent and immediate relevance for our everyday lives is what is called *soe pa* in Tibetan. Though usually translated as patience, *soe pa* also includes the virtues of tolerance, forbearance, and forgiveness. What it really means is the ability to endure suffering. It entails not giving in to our instinctive urge to respond negatively to our difficulties. But *soe pa* has nothing to do with being either passive or impotent. It is not a case of tolerating something just because you do not have the ability to hit back. Nor is it enduring injustice grudgingly, through gritted teeth. Instead, genuine patience requires great strength. It is fundamentally the exercise of restraint based on mental discipline. There are three aspects of patience, or forbearance, to consider: forbearance toward those who harm us, acceptance of suffering, and acceptance of reality.

PATIENCE TOWARD THE PERPETRATORS OF HARM

As I have already suggested, reflecting on the fact that everything depends on a great many causes and conditions can do much to help us tolerate the wrongs inflicted on us by others. When people injure us in some way, it is helpful to recall that a vast array of factors will have contributed to their behavior. When we face aggression or disrespect, it is worth considering why the aggressive or disrespectful people are acting that way. Very likely, their behavior reflects difficulties they themselves are experiencing. Recognizing this can moderate our instinct to retaliate.

It is also useful to remember that anger is not something anyone actually wants. When we ourselves get angry, for example, is it because we want to? No. It comes upon us involuntarily. Like falling ill, becoming angry is not something we do deliberately. Furthermore, given that the perpetrators of the harm are just like me and you, human beings who aspire to happiness and wish to avoid suffering, they too are deserving of our compassion and concern. Kindness and forgiveness are therefore much more appropriate responses to hostility than anger.

As with the exercise of forgiveness, we need to distinguish between the act and the actor, between the harmful deed and the person who committed it. While remaining firm in our opposition to the unjust act itself, we can still retain our sense of concern and compassion for the perpetrator of that harm.

PATIENCE THROUGH ACCEPTANCE OF SUFFERING

An important dimension of the practice of patience or forbearance is the cultivation of greater acceptance of suffering and difficulties, which are, in fact, unavoidable parts of our existence. This training in patience takes the form of developing a genuine attitude of acceptance of the reality that life involves hardship. To be in denial about suffering or to expect life to be easy only causes a person additional misery. I do not mean to suggest that suffering is somehow good in itself; I simply mean that accepting it will make it easier to bear.

Traveling the world, I have noticed that people in less developed countries, whose lives are hard in material terms, often seem more contented than those in more affluent countries, who have relatively easy lives. Beneath the outward affluence in materially advanced societies lies a good deal of inner anxiety and dissatisfaction, while in poorer countries I am often struck by the simple joy one often encounters. How to account for this? It seems that hardship, in forcing us to exercise greater patience and forbearance in life, actually makes us stronger and more robust. From the daily experience of hardship comes a greater capacity for accepting difficulties without losing an inner sense of calm. This is something I have also observed in some of my European friends. Those of my own generation, who lived through the hardships of the Second World War, seem to possess greater forbearance and strength of character than the younger generations who have never encountered such difficulties. The experience of losing friends and family, living with uncertainty, and making do on meager rations has, it seems, made that generation tougher. They are more able to cope with adversity without losing their humor. Of course I do not want to advocate hardship as a way of life, but merely to show that, if you relate to hardship constructively, by seeing its benefits, it can bring you inner strength or fortitude.

How, though, are we to deal with the ordinary setbacks of life? Again I find the advice of Shantideva, the eighth-century Indian thinker, especially helpful.

If there is a solution,
Then what need is there for dejection?
If there is no solution,
Then what point is there in dejection?

I call this the "no need, no point" approach to dealing with problems. If a problem has a solution, then it should not be a cause for excessive worry. Rather than feeling overwhelmed, we should simply work with determination to reach the solution. If after careful consideration we conclude that there is no solution to be found, we gain nothing by worrying. Instead, the sooner we accept that the problem cannot be rectified, the easier it will be to carry on with our lives. Either way, there is no point in excessive worrying! Not only does it do us no good, but it can severely harm us by making us weaker, or worse, it can lead to depression.

Of course this is not to suggest that we should *surrender* to suffering. On the contrary, *accepting* suffering, far from being a surrender, is the first step toward combating its harm. By accepting hardship, we begin to see that it is not entirely negative. It can, for example, be a powerful force in bringing us together with others by enlivening our empathetic, compassionate natures. Above all, suffering helps us recognize our kinship with one another. And with this recognition, we are no longer overwhelmed by our own difficulties, but gain the strength we need to meet the challenges we face.

Personal suffering can also be a catalyst for individual spiritual growth. In addition to making us stronger, it can bring us a kind of humility and help us to be more in tune with reality. These effects of suffering are recognized by all the world's major religious traditions. They are also something I have felt in my own life. I am in no doubt that my experience of exile has given me a deeper understanding of life than I would have if I were still living in Tibet as the privileged ruler of a country.

PATIENCE THROUGH CONTEMPLATION OF REALITY

The third dimension of the practice of patience involves focusing on those facets of reality which we, as individuals, have the most difficulty in accepting. These may include, for example, aging or death. These topics are often regarded as taboo because many people just do not want to think about them. This seems to be particularly the case in more affluent societies, where consumerism promotes the culture of youth. And yet contemplating such topics can enhance our well-being. Reflecting deeply upon the inevitability of old age and death and their roles as parts of our existence can lead us to greater tolerance toward these aspects of reality, which otherwise might cause us despair and dejection.

As I have already suggested several times, everything in the world comes about as a result of many factors. In any given occurrence, our own actions are only one factor in a great range of causes and conditions. Similarly, there are always many sides to any situation. When, therefore, we suffer some misfortune, such as not getting the job we hoped for, it is worth considering that the same decision that disappointed us will have benefited someone else, perhaps someone in even greater need. Though not easy, such considerations can temper our sense of loss with some sympathetic joy at others' good fortune. At the same time, the simple act of moving the focus of our attention away from ourselves will have the effect of making the problem appear less unbearable.

The benefits of cultivating patience are obvious. The practice of patience guards us against loss of composure and, in doing so, enables us to exercise discernment, even in the heat of difficult situations. It gives us inner space. And within that space we gain a degree of self-control, which allows us to choose to respond to situations in an appropriate and compassionate manner rather than being driven by our compulsions. With constant cultivation, patience as I have described it equips us to deal with life's inevitable ups and downs. What is more, there is no doubt that patience is a quality that others appreciate tremendously! Through exercising patience, we naturally become far more appealing to others. It helps put people at ease in our presence and causes them to enjoy our company. But above all, patience is a powerful antidote to the destructive emotions of anger and frustration.

Contentment

On my earliest trips to western countries, I sometimes used to visit shopping malls. In those days there were no such malls in India, and it was impressive to us Tibetans to see all the smart shops with their window displays lit up with of all kinds of consumer products. Ever since childhood I have had a love of mechanical objects like watches, so I found the modern mechanical and electronic gadgets in these stores most attractive. Looking at them, I would sometimes think, "Oh, I would like this," "I would like that." But then I would ask myself, "Do I really need it?" Of course, most of the time, the answer was no. So my first thoughts were coming from some kind of instinctive greed; but as soon as I checked myself and took a realistic view, I no longer felt any need to acquire or control those items. This is what I understand by the application of contentment.

Referring to contentment as a key ethical value sometimes creates a little confusion. One might say that contentment is not itself an ethical value, since it concerns one's own well-being rather than that of others. Isn't contentment what underlies the happiness that comes through living with a compassionate concern for others? If so, how can it be regarded as an ethical value to be nurtured in its own right? Moreover, one might say, contentment can't be practiced; it has to be arrived at.

When I talk about contentment as an ethical value in this way, what I am really talking about is not a general state of well-being or happiness, but a more specific notion of contentment which in Tibetan we call *chogshé.* I do not know of any simple translation of this term in English or any other western language, and since it is generally translated as "contentment," I also use that term. However, what *chogshé* really means is an *absence of greed.* Literally it means "knowing [what is] enough" or "knowing when to be contented." It means being able to find satisfaction without looking for more.

So contentment, according to this view, is something like the virtue of moderation. It implies a certain modesty of ambition, or having limited desires. By living modestly and setting reasonable limits, we free ourselves from the sense of insecurity and insufficiency born of incessant craving. By practicing contentment, we allow ourselves to rest in an underlying state of satisfaction, confident in the knowledge that we are living by the ideals we seek to uphold. By limiting our wants and desires, we avoid suffering the dissatisfaction and frustration which greed generates.

There is a saying in Tibetan that "at the door of the miserable rich man sleeps the contented beggar." The point is not that poverty is a virtue, but that happiness comes not from wealth but from setting limits on our desires and living within those limits with satisfaction.

Cultivating contentment is especially important, I feel, in today's materialistic world of global consumerism. Materialistic society puts people under constant pressure to want more and to spend more long after their basic needs are satisfied. Sophisticated advertising is designed to excite the imagination and to generate a perception that material goods will make us happy, and that we are somehow lacking unless we acquire the latest accessory, gadget, or fashion item. The materialism of modern society therefore makes the practice of moderation and contentment a daily necessity if we are to resist succumbing to a sense of personal dissatisfaction born of unrealistic craving.

Controlling our desire for more, learning to live within realistic limits, is not only in our own individual interest. It is also necessary if we are to overcome the challenges to life on Earth that our incessant quest for more generates. The material resources of this planet are finite. Add the facts that the global population is rising rapidly and that those in the less developed countries naturally aspire to the same level of comfort enjoyed in the developed world, as is their right, and it becomes clear that our present path is unsustainable. The world's great natural spaces do much to maintain the environmental equilibrium of the planet. Yet forests, oceans, and other natural environments are being encroached on and destroyed, and during my own lifetime many species of animals and plants have become extinct. So the comfortable modern lifestyles that many of us take for granted and many others aspire to actually come at a considerable cost.

The need for contentment is painfully illustrated by the recent financial crisis, the repercussions of which are still being felt across our deeply interdependent world. It is easy to blame politicians for failing to sufficiently regulate financial institutions. Ultimately, though, this crisis was generated by greed itself—by the failure to exercise appropriate moderation and restraint in the blind quest for ever-greater profits. Also, as an Italian businessman explained to me, there was excessive speculation. The word "speculation" itself means acting without full knowledge. In this case, the level of caution and humility appropriate to actions undertaken without full knowledge was clearly absent. Here the problem was essentially one of arrogance and shortsightedness. A third issue was the lack of transparency, which allowed dishonesty and deceit to thrive unchecked. There was nothing inevitable about any of these factors. They are all simple ethical failings, chief among which is greed. And the only effective antidote to greed is moderation and contentment.

Of course, in extolling the benefits of simplicity and modesty, I am not suggesting that poverty is acceptable. On the contrary, poverty is a tremendous hardship, one that we must do all we can to end. In addition to making survival a struggle, poverty tends to disempower people and make them feel cowed or demoralized. It can lead to profound mental distress and rob people of any opportunity for improvement of their economic situation. In these ways, it makes the poor suffer greatly. On the personal level, however, the sooner we accept that riches alone do not bring happiness, and the sooner we learn to live with a sense of modesty, the better off we will be, especially with respect to our happiness.

Time and geography will always impose limits on how much wealth anyone can succeed in accruing in a single lifetime. Given this natural limit, it seems wiser to set one's own limits through the exercise of contentment. In contrast, when it comes to acquiring mental riches, the potential is limitless. Here, where there is no natural limit, it is appropriate *not* to be contented with what you have, but to constantly strive for more. Unfortunately, most of us do the exact opposite. We are never quite satisfied with what we have materially, but we tend to be thoroughly complacent about our mental riches.

Self-Discipline

Closely connected to the value of contentment is that of self-discipline. In fact, the value of contentment presupposes the exercise of some degree of self-discipline, as indeed do all the inner values discussed in this book.

The important point about the virtue of self-discipline is that it must be voluntarily embraced. When discipline is imposed from the outside, it is very rarely effective and sometimes can even be counterproductive. When discipline is imposed by fear, either fear of some external authority or fear stemming from our own cultural or religious conditioning, the individual often feels very little enthusiasm for it. As a result, imposed discipline rarely brings about inner transformation.

On the other hand, if we adopt self-regulation voluntarily, out of appreciation of its value and the benefits of refraining from bad habits, it is only natural for us to undertake it with greater determination. This in turn makes our self-discipline more enduring.

In order to cultivate such voluntarily embraced self-discipline, we must once again take time to appreciate and dwell upon its many benefits, not just for ourselves, but also for others and even for humanity at large. By doing this, we can generate the enthusiasm required to maintain our motivation and determination.

It is useful to begin by reflecting on the harm we do to ourselves, even physically, when we succumb to temptation and bad habits. Then we can also consider the harm that our bad habits inflict on others. It is easy to assume that our personal behavior and habits have no real effect on others, but this is seldom the case. Suppose, for example, that one member of a family is addicted to drugs. Although, of course, the other family members will not suffer the direct physical and mental ill effects of the drug, this does not mean they will not be harmed. In all likelihood they will be deeply afflicted by worry and concern, as well as by whatever other agonies and complications may accompany the situation. So, when considering the harm we inflict through a lack of self-discipline in our personal habits, we should always be mindful of those who care about our welfare, and whose welfare is intimately connected to our own.

It can also be useful to consider the harmful effects of a lack of self-discipline at a wider social level. In my view, the problem of corruption, which is prevalent in so many parts of the world, is actually nothing but a failure of self-discipline. Corruption is always a surrender to self-serving attitudes of greed, bias, and dishonesty. Even the existence of a fair and just legal system becomes of little value when that system is paralyzed by corruption.

With the awareness that comes from contemplating the consequences of a lack of self-discipline, we can gradually develop a greater ability to resist temptation in our own life. Eventually, with sustained practice, self-discipline will start to come naturally and will no longer require conscious effort and willpower. At that point, when restraint and moderation come naturally, we begin to feel the great sense of freedom that comes with self-mastery. This virtue of self-discipline is extolled in all the world's major religious traditions. In Islam, for example, a strong emphasis is placed on the virtue of *sabr*—steadfastness, self-control, patience, or fortitude—and those who have this quality, the *sabireen,* are said to be beloved of God.

Gaining mastery over our destructive propensities through the exercise of awareness and self-discipline at the levels of body, speech, and mind frees us from the inner turmoil that naturally arises when our behavior is at odds with our ideals. In place of this turmoil come confidence, integrity, and dignity—heroic qualities all humans naturally aspire to.

Generosity

It seems worthwhile to say a few words about the value of generosity. Generosity is the most natural outward expression of an inner attitude of compassion and loving-kindness. When one desires to alleviate the suffering of others and to promote their well-being, then generosity—in action, word, and thought—is this desire put into practice.

It is important to recognize that "generosity" here refers not just to giving in a material sense, but to generosity of the heart. As such, it is closely connected to the virtue of forgiveness. Without generosity of the heart, genuine forgiveness is impossible.

Classical Buddhist texts describe generosity in terms of four kinds of giving: first, the giving of material goods; second, the giving of freedom from fear, which means offering safety and security to others and dealing with them honestly; third, the giving of spiritual counsel, which entails offering comfort, concern, and advice to support others' psychological and emotional well-being; and fourth, the giving of love.

An important point to recognize at the outset is that the aim of any of these four kinds of giving should never be to ingratiate oneself with others, but should always be to benefit the recipient. If one's motivation is in any way connected to seeking one's own benefit, this is not genuine generosity.

Classical Buddhist texts also note the need to be discerning when engaging in acts of generosity. For example, in addition to ensuring the soundness of one's motivation, they discuss the need to be aware of specific contexts in which giving might not be appropriate. Giving disproportionately, or giving to someone at a wrong time, might do the recipient more harm than good. And clearly there are certain items, such as poisons or weapons, which are, by their very nature, inappropriate for giving. If what we give is likely to be used to harm others, the principle of compassion dictates that we shun giving in that context. Furthermore, these texts emphasize the need to be sure we are giving out of respect for the recipient, not out of a sense of superiority. A genuine act of generosity will honor the recipient's dignity. These, I think, are all helpful instructions for us to keep in mind.

Charitable Giving and Philanthropy

A few years ago, I took part in an interesting panel discussion in New York on the subject of philanthropy. So far as charitable giving is concerned, the most pressing areas of need, in my view, are those of health and education. Health is essential to human dignity and well-being, but the resources required for modern health care are simply unavailable to many in the world. Education provides the means by which people can gain the skills and resourcefulness required to escape poverty.

Charitable giving is particularly emphasized in the Abrahamic faiths, in which giving to the needy is regarded as an important religious obligation. I have often been impressed by the charitable work undertaken, much of it by Christian charities, in the developing world. We Tibetans, especially during the difficult early years of our exile, have ourselves been on the receiving end of this generosity, and have directly felt its benefit. In Islam, almsgiving or *zakaat* is considered one of the five pillars that every devout person must practice, and in Judaism, too, charitable giving is held to be a key component of religious observance.

But charitable giving does not just benefit the recipients. On the part of donors, what could possibly be more gratifying than the knowledge that, through their own help, many others — real people with real needs — are being benefited?

For those who are already rich, additional wealth beyond a certain level does not bring them any real value, unless they put this wealth to good use. Even a billionaire has the same size of stomach as anyone else; and the number of homes one person can live in is finite. After a certain point, greater luxury and extravagance have no real effect on one's level of comfort. Eventually wealth becomes merely a series of figures on paper or on a computer screen. Furthermore, if one cares about moral principles or about maintaining a basic sense of decency, then indulging in an excessive lifestyle for oneself in the face of all the poverty that exists in the world can be problematic. It is a bit like a person eating a meal with a sense of abandon in front of a beggar who is dying of hunger!

Fortunately, there are today some remarkable people who, through their philanthropic activity, share their enormous wealth with the needy and the poor in many parts of the world, especially in the fields of health and education. I have already mentioned Bill and Melinda Gates, who, through their charity work, dedicate so much to others. I also know personally the wonderful philanthropic work of Pierre and Pamela Omidyar, who contribute a substantial part of their wealth to helping others. When I meet such individuals I always express my appreciation of their generosity toward the world's needy. I therefore appeal once again to all those who are in similar positions of wealth, to seriously consider sharing their resources with others through philanthropy.

Yet it is not just the extremely wealthy who need to think seriously about giving. Even for those of limited means, an attitude of generosity has huge benefits, in opening one's heart and bringing one a sense of sympathetic joy and connection to others. Giving material goods is one form of generosity, but one can extend an attitude of generosity into all one's behavior. Being kind, attentive, and honest in dealings with others, offering praise where it is due, giving comfort and advice where they are needed, and simply sharing one's time with someone—all these are forms of generosity, and they do not require any particular level of material wealth.

Joy in Giving

An important aspect of the practice of generosity, I feel, is to take joy in it. In the classical Indian tradition, there is a custom of dedicating acts of generosity to a higher altruistic goal. This helps ensure that generosity is not blind, or driven by partiality or bias, but is directed toward the greater good of all humanity. The custom of dedication also allows the giver to rejoice in the act of giving. Taking joy in giving is very helpful, since it makes us more inclined to engage in similar acts of kindness and charity in the future.

The great thing about giving is that it not only benefits the recipient but also brings profound benefits to the giver. And the more one gives, the more one enjoys giving.

11

Meditation as Mental Cultivation

WE HAVE NOW explored in some detail what spirituality and ethical living entail in terms of personal practice. We have discussed some ways to bring mindful awareness into everyday life, some ways to develop greater awareness so that we can learn to regulate our emotions, and, finally, some ways to actively cultivate our inner values. Since all these practices, especially the last two, involve some degree of disciplined application of the mind, in this final chapter I would like to say a few words about cultivating mental discipline. For myself, such cultivation is an indispensable part of daily life. On the one hand, it helps reinforce my determination always to act compassionately for the well-being of others. On the other, it helps me keep in check those afflictive thoughts and emotions by which we are all assailed from time to time, and to maintain a calm mind.

By mental cultivation I mean a disciplined application of mind that involves deepening our familiarity with a chosen object or theme. Here I am thinking of the Sanskrit term *bhavana,* which connotes "cultivation," and whose Tibetan equivalent, *gom,* has the connotation of "familiarization." These two terms, often translated into English as *meditation,* refer to a whole range of mental practices and not just, as many suppose, to simple methods of relaxation. The original terms imply a process of cultivating familiarity with something, whether it is a habit, a way of seeing, or a way of being.

A *Process of Transformation*

How, then, does this process of mental cultivation lead to spiritual and inner transformation? Here it may be helpful to invoke the idea of the "three levels of understanding," as found in the classical Buddhist theory of mental transformation. These levels are understanding derived through hearing (or learning), understanding derived through reflection, and understanding derived through contemplative experience. For example, consider people who are seeking to understand the deeply interdependent nature of today's world. They may first learn about it by listening to someone talk about this issue or by reading about it. But unless they deeply reflect upon what they hear or read, their understanding remains superficial and closely tied to their knowledge of the meaning of the words. At this level, their understanding of a given fact will be only an informed assumption. However, as they then reflect more deeply upon its meaning, applying analysis as well as dwelling mindfully upon the conclusion they reach, a deep sense of conviction arises of the truth of the fact. This is the second level in the process of understanding. Finally, as they continue to cultivate deep familiarity with the fact, their insight into it becomes internalized, making it almost part of their own nature. They have then reached the third level of understanding, which is characterized in the classical texts as experiential, spontaneous, and effortless.

There is nothing mysterious about this process of transformation. In fact, it is something that occurs in our everyday lives. A good analogy is the process of acquiring a skill, such as swimming or riding a bicycle, where the key factor is actual practice. In the context of education, for example, this progression—from first hearing or learning, to deepening one's understanding through critical reflection, to conviction—is quite usual. It is well known, for instance, that knowledge that is based simply on hearing or reading, without being processed through reflection, does not lead to strong conviction. For this reason it cannot result in any real change. But if, through critical reflection, we have gained deep conviction about what we have learned, this can lead to a serious commitment on our part to make that knowledge part of our personal outlook.

This process applies not just to the development of the intellect but also to that of our more affective qualities, such as compassion. Through critical reflection we come to recognize the value of compassion. This can in turn lead to a profound admiration of the virtue itself. Admiration of the virtue may then lead to a commitment to cultivate compassion within ourselves, and this commitment, to actual practice. In other words, awareness of the benefits gives rise to conviction that it is worthwhile to practice, and practice leads us to actually realize, or bring into being, the quality or virtue we began by reflecting on.

Forms of Mental Cultivation

All the major faith traditions emphasize the importance of developing one's inner life, and many of the techniques found in my own tradition exist in some form in other traditions as well. In particular, there are many similarities between the various mental training practices used in different Indian contemplative traditions. But large areas are shared with other spiritual traditions too. Recently, for example, I attended a very enjoyable and informative talk on contemplative prayer given by a Christian Carmelite monk who pointed out some striking similarities between Christian and Buddhist techniques.

Yet, for all the associations of meditation or mental cultivation with religion, there is no reason why it should not be undertaken in an entirely secular context. After all, mental discipline itself requires no faith commitment. All it requires is a recognition that developing a calmer, clearer mind is a worthwhile endeavor and an understanding that doing so will benefit both oneself and others. So far as my own daily practice is concerned, besides certain specifically religious and devotional exercises, I engage in two main types of mental cultivation practice—*discursive* or *analytic* meditation and *absorptive* meditation. The first is a kind of analytic process by means of which the meditator engages in a series of reflections, while the second involves concentrating on a specific object or objective and placing one's mind upon it as if dwelling deeply on a conclusion. I find that combining the two techniques is most beneficial.

One useful way to understand the different forms of mental cultivation is to look at each practice from the perspective of its objective. There is, for example, the practice which has the form of *taking something as an object,* such as when one takes, say, the fundamental equality of all beings as the object of deep contemplation. Then there is meditation in the form of *cultivation of positive mental qualities.* In this form, qualities like compassion and loving-kindness are not so much seen as the objects of the practice. Rather, the person seeks to cultivate these qualities within his or her heart. The first of these two approaches corresponds to the development of mental states that are more cognitively oriented, such as understanding, while the second develops more affect-oriented mental states, such as compassion. We might refer to these two processes as "educating our mind" and "educating our heart."

Because we live in an age when much can be done at the touch of a button, some of us may expect to see immediate change in the domain of mental cultivation as well. We may suppose that inner transformation is simply a matter of getting the correct formula or reciting the right mantra. This is a mistake. Mental cultivation takes time and effort and involves hard work and sustained dedication.

Dealing with Procrastination

For the beginner, the first requirement for mental cultivation is a serious commitment to practice. Without such a commitment, it is unlikely that a person will ever get around to starting at all! I sometimes tell a story in connection with the problem of procrastination. There was once a lama who, to encourage his students, promised he would take them on a picnic one day. This incentive had the hoped-for effect, and the young monks eagerly applied themselves to their studies. Yet the promised picnic did not materialize. After some time, the youngest student, not willing to let go of the prospect of a day off, reminded the teacher of his promise. The lama responded by saying he was too busy at the moment, so it would have to wait awhile. A long time passed, and summer gave way to autumn. Again the student reminded the lama, "When are we going on this famous picnic?" Again the lama replied, "Not just now, I'm really far too busy." One day the lama noticed a commotion among the students. "What is happening?" he asked. A dead body was being carried out of the monastery. "Well," replied the youngest student, "that poor man over there is going on a picnic!"

The point of this story is that unless we make time and a proper commitment for the things we tell ourselves and others we are going to do, we will always have other obligations and more pressing concerns—while death may intervene at any time.

Planning Our Practice

At the outset I should sound a note of caution. As the beginning meditator will quickly discover, the mind is like a wild horse. Like a wild horse, it takes a long time as well as familiarity with the person who wishes to tame it before it will settle down and obey commands. Similarly, only with gentle persistence over an extended period will the real benefits of meditation become apparent. Of course it is all right to set aside just a few days to try out a short program of mental training, but it is wrong to judge the results before you have really given it a chance. It may take months, even years, to realize its full benefits.

As to the specifics of practice, early morning is generally the best time of day. At that time, the mind is at its freshest and clearest. However, it is important to remember that if you are to practice well in the early morning, you need to have had a good night's sleep beforehand. For myself, I must say that I have been most fortunate when it comes to sleep. Despite rising every morning around 3:30 A.M., on average I make sure that I get eight or nine hours of sound sleep. For a lot of people, this may be difficult to arrange. If, for example, there are young children in the house, it may not be possible to meditate during the early hours. If this is the case, it will probably be better to find some other time to practice, preferably after a short nap or when the children are out of the house. I should also point out that the mind will tend to be sluggish if you have eaten a lot beforehand. Ideally you should not eat too much in the evening if you hope to practice well the following morning.

As to the amount of time you should aim to set aside for meditation, in the early stages even ten to fifteen minutes per session is quite adequate. In fact, it is much better to have modest ambitions than to embark on an unsustainable program which is more likely to put you off than to help you ingrain a habit. It is also helpful to plan to practice for a few minutes several times during the day in addition to the main session. As you keep a fire going by stoking it every so often, you can maintain the continuum of your meditation by "topping up" every now and again so that what you gained earlier does not fade away entirely by the time you begin the next proper session.

Regarding where to practice, it is said in the classical training manuals that sound is like a thorn in the mind. For most people, therefore, it is very helpful to find somewhere to sit where we will not be disturbed by noise. Obviously, too, it is a good idea to switch off the telephone before starting. But none of this is to say that meditation cannot be practiced more or less anywhere, or at any moment of the day. I am talking here just about the ideal. Personally, I find it a good use of time to meditate when traveling.

As to the physical posture appropriate for meditation, any position that is comfortable will do, though if you become *too* comfortable, there is a danger that you may drift off to sleep. That said, it can be helpful to adopt what is usually called the lotus position, in which you cross your legs with each foot resting on the opposite thigh. One advantage of this position is that, in addition to keeping you warm, it keeps your back quite straight. At first it may be uncomfortable, in which case simply sitting with your legs crossed some of the time is all right, as indeed is sitting on a chair if that position is also difficult. Similarly, for those who, on account of their faith tradition, prefer to meditate while kneeling, that too is all right. You should choose whatever position you find least distracting.

If you do choose the lotus position, you can place your hands in a relaxed position, with the back of the right hand resting on the palm of the left. Allow the elbows to rest loosely, pushed out a bit from the body so that there is a gap which the air can pass through. Often it is helpful to sit on a cushion which is raised slightly at the back. This helps straighten the backbone, which ideally should be kept straight as an arrow, with just the neck bent a little downward. Keeping the tip of the tongue touching the palate helps prevent the thirst which can set in as a result of certain breathing exercises. The lips and teeth can be left as usual. So far as the eyes are concerned, you can discover for yourself what position works best for you. Some people find that meditating with their eyes open is most effective. Others find this very distracting. For most, half-closing the eyes is generally best, but some find it helpful to close them completely.

Relaxing and Settling the Mind

Once you are settled, the first thing to do is take a few deep breaths. Then, breathing normally again, try to focus on your breath, noticing the air as it enters and leaves through the nostrils. What you are trying to achieve is a mind in a neutral state, neither positive nor negative. Alternatively, you can take one inhalation and one exhalation while silently counting from one to five or seven, and then repeat the process a few times. The advantage of this silent counting is that, in giving our mind a task to perform, it makes it less likely to be swept away by extraneous thoughts. In either case, spending a few minutes just observing your breathing is usually a good way to achieve a calmer mental state.

We can liken this process of settling the mind to dyeing a piece of cloth. White cloth can easily be dyed a different color, but it is difficult to dye a piece of cloth that is already colored, unless we want to make it black. In the same way, when the mind is agitated, a positive result is hard to come by.

Sometimes you may find it difficult to concentrate at all because your mind is in the grip of some powerful emotion, like anger. At such times, it can be helpful to quietly say a few words over and over. A formula such as "I let go of my afflictive emotions" or, for religious believers, a short devotional prayer or mantra repeated a few times can loosen the grip of the emotion. If this technique does not work, then maybe you need to get up and go for a short walk before trying again.

There may be occasions, especially in the beginning stages, when negative thoughts keep returning after a short time. In such cases, you may find that a whole session is taken up with exercises to calm or still the mind. This is all right: it is still mental training. As you gain some experience of how the mind works and learn what techniques work best for you, you will gradually become familiar with a more neutral state of mind. This alone is good progress.

When you have succeeded in establishing a more settled state, perhaps a few minutes into your session, you can then begin the actual work of mental cultivation.

In the initial stages of your training, it is best to practice several different exercises successively. To start with, you may find it impossible to keep your mind focused for more than a few minutes—perhaps even just a few seconds—at a time before distraction sets in. This is quite normal. As soon as you realize you have become distracted, just return gently to whatever you were doing before the distraction arose. There should be no anger or self-reproach when this happens, just a patient recognition of what the mind is doing and a calm redirection of the attention. The important thing is not to become discouraged.

Reflecting on the Benefits of Mental Training

One very useful exercise at the beginning of a session is to consider the benefits of practice. An immediate benefit is that practice gives us a brief respite from the often obsessive worrying, calculating, and fantasizing with which our minds are habitually occupied. This by itself is a great boon. Another benefit to reflect on is that practice is a sure path to the highest wisdom, even if that path is a long one and there will be many obstacles to overcome along the way.

It is also good to spend some time reflecting on what may happen if we neglect to practice. There is a danger that we will end up like the monk in the picnic story—carried off as a corpse—before we ever know the benefits of the endeavor. One who never engages in this kind of work has very little chance of dealing effectively with the destructive thoughts and emotions which, when they take hold of us, destroy all hope of peace of mind.

Having deeply considered these two opposing possibilities and the advantages of the one compared with the disadvantages of the other, we then go back and forth between them. As we do so, we should find that the benefits far outweigh any arguments in favor of not practicing. We then rest the mind on this conclusion for a short time before moving on to the next stage of the session.

Some Formal Practices

FOCUSED ATTENTION

A more formal meditation practice is the cultivation of sustained attention through single-pointed concentration. Here, you choose an object as the focus of your attention. It may be a flower, a painting, or simply an orb of light; or, for a religious practitioner, a sacred object such as a crucifix or an image of a Buddha. Although, when you begin, it may be helpful to have the actual object in front of you as an aid, ultimately the physical thing is not the focus of your attention. Instead, once you have chosen your object, try to cultivate a mental image of it, and when you are quite familiar with the image, you fix it in your mind's eye. This mental image of the object is what serves as the anchor for your meditation.

Having relaxed and settled your mind, try to maintain your focus on the object. Visualize it about four feet in front of you and at the level of your eyebrows. Imagine the object to be approximately two inches in height and radiating light, so that the image is bright and clear. Also try to conceive of it as being heavy. This heaviness has the effect of preventing excitement, while the object's brightness prevents the onset of laxity.

It is best, when engaging in this type of meditation, not to shut the eyes but to keep them slightly open, looking downwards. Sometimes they may close of their own accord, and that is all right. But the important thing is that they should be neither tightly closed nor wide open. I might also mention here that for people who, like me, normally wear glasses, taking them off for meditating is not always a good idea. Although without our glasses there is less danger of visual distraction, we may, owing to the loss of visual clarity, more easily experience laxity or dullness. This in turn can lead to our practice taking the form of an undirected reverie. If this happens, one helpful countermeasure is to think of something agreeable, something that makes you feel joyful. Another is to think of something sobering, even something that makes you feel a little sad. Or you may imagine looking down from a mountaintop where you have an unimpeded view in every direction.

If you start to suffer the opposite problem—being distracted by something you see—you need to try to withdraw the mind from the eyes. Sitting in front of a blank wall can be helpful in such circumstances.

When the object you are visualizing is stable in your mind's eye—perhaps after many, many weeks or months of persistent practice—you now try to inspect the mind itself as it holds the object in view. Here you are trying to focus the mind but at the same time to inspect it, as from a corner, to ensure that you are not inadvertently letting it become too relaxed. When your mind becomes too relaxed, sleep may not be far off! But when you succeed in generating a strong and clear mental image, you can start to familiarize yourself with the sort of focus that in ordinary life you may only experience when attempting to solve a particularly challenging mental problem. The idea here is that when you have learned to really focus the mind, then, rather in the same way that water is channeled through a hydroelectric plant to generate the great force required to drive the turbines, you can use the whole force of your mind to focus on qualities such as compassion, patience, tolerance, and forgiveness.

Even after you achieve some ability to maintain focus, inevitably you will find yourself losing attention from time to time as your mind wanders away from your object, either because of external events or because of internal thought processes. When you notice that your mind has wandered away, consciously recognize this and gently bring it back to the object. If necessary, every now and then, refresh your visualization of the object so that your image of it regains its clarity. Two qualities are essential in this kind of meditation: mental clarity and stability. Mental clarity assists you in maintaining your focus. Stability assists you in ensuring clarity by monitoring whether or not your attention remains vibrant. To help ensure the continued presence of these two qualities, you need to develop and then to apply two important faculties, those pertaining to mindfulness and introspective awareness. It is through constant application of these two faculties that you can gradually learn to train your focus so that you become capable of sustaining your attention for a prolonged period of time.

To summarize, then: in a typical formal session, we begin by settling our mind through breathing. We then choose our object of meditation and focus our attention on it, now and then monitoring whether our attention has been distracted. When we notice our mind wandering, we gently bring it back to our object of meditation and continue. Finally, when we wish to end our session, we can do some deep breathing exercises once again so that we finish in a relaxed state of mind.

PRESENT-MOMENT AWARENESS

With your mind quite relaxed through some form of breathing exercise, another useful practice is to try to rest your mind in, as it were, its natural state of basic awareness, or what we can call "present-moment awareness." When you begin, it is important to set a forceful intention not to allow your mind to be swept away by thoughts of what might happen in the future or recollections of things that have happened in the past. Instead, establish the intention to place your mind simply on the present moment and to keep it there as long as possible. When undertaking this practice, it is a good idea to sit, if possible, facing a wall that has no striking color or pattern. Then, after several deep breaths, you simply rest the mind and start to observe it.

This is actually quite a difficult thing to do at first. In our everyday life, our mental world is dominated by object-oriented states, either in the form of sensory experiences or in the form of thoughts, memories, and ideas. Very rarely do we experience a state that is not tied to specific content but simply rests in the mind's natural state of awareness. So, when you initially engage in this meditation, inevitably you will find that your mind wanders off, thoughts and images float through your conscious awareness, or a memory pops up for no apparent reason. When this happens, do not get caught up in the energy of these thoughts and images by trying to suppress or reinforce them. Simply observe them and let them go, as if they are clouds appearing in the sky and fading from view, or bubbles arising and dissolving back into water. Over time, you will begin to catch glimpses of your mind's basic state of awareness, or of what could be called its "mere luminosity." As you proceed in this way, every now and then you will come to experience short intervals of what feels like an absence or a vacuum, when your mind has no particular content. Your first successes in this will only be fleeting. But with persistence over a long period, what begins as a glimpse can gradually be extended, and you can start to understand that the mind is like a mirror, or clear water, in which images appear and disappear without affecting the medium in which they appear.

One important benefit of this practice is the skill you gain of being able to observe your thoughts without being drawn into them. Like a detached onlooker watching a spectacle, you will learn how to see your thoughts for what they are, namely constructs of your mind. So many of our problems arise because, in our naive untrained state, we confuse our thoughts with actual reality. We seize on the content of our thoughts as real and build our entire perception and response to reality on it. In so doing, we tie ourselves ever tighter into a world that is essentially our own creation and become trapped in it, like a length of rope entangled in its own knots.

TRAINING IN COMPASSION AND LOVING-KINDNESS

Another very beneficial class of practices involves cultivating positive mental qualities, such as compassion and loving-kindness. These types of exercises make use of deliberate thought processes. Once again, we begin with a preliminary breathing exercise to relax and settle the mind. Only after that preparation do we begin the actual practice.

These exercises are particularly useful for occasions when you are struggling with your attitude or feelings toward a person with whom you have difficulty. First, bring that person into your mind, conjuring up a vivid image so that you almost feel his or her presence. Next, start to contemplate the fact that he or she also has hopes and dreams, feels joy when things go well and feels sadness when they do not. In this, there is not an iota of difference between the other person and yourself. Just like you, this person wishes for happiness and does not want suffering.

Recognizing this shared fundamental aspiration, try to feel connected with the person and cultivate the wish that he or she achieve happiness. It may be helpful if you silently repeat the wish in words, saying something like "May you be free of suffering and its causes. May you attain happiness and peace." Then rest your mind in this state of compassion. Of the two types of mental cultivation practice mentioned earlier, discursive and absorptive, this way of cultivating compassion primarily involves a discursive process, but every now and then it is also good to rest the mind in a state of absorption, somewhat in the fashion of bringing home a concluding point in the course of an argument.

Since I have already discussed the topic of compassion at some length, I shall not elaborate further here. Many of the points outlined earlier can be brought into your deliberate cultivation of compassion. And this combination of methods—of discursive mental training interspersed with absorptive mental training—is equally useful in the cultivation of other inner qualities, such as patience or forbearance.

CULTIVATING EQUANIMITY

In referring to the state of equanimity, it is important not to confuse this with indifference. Rather, equanimity is a state of mind where one relates to others in a way that is free of prejudice rooted in the afflictions of excessive attraction or aversion.

There are two principal forms of equanimity practice. One is likened to leveling out garden soil so that the flowers we plant grow evenly and well. Here the aim is to curb our habitual tendency to define our interactions with others in terms of self-referential categories of friends, foes, and strangers. The second practice is about developing, as it were, a gut-level recognition of the fundamental equality of self and others as human beings who aspire to happiness and wish to avoid suffering.

In the first of these practices, we again employ discursive thought processes. Although it is normal to feel close to our loved ones, negative toward those who wish us harm, and indifferent toward strangers, too often we create unnecessary problems and suffering, for ourselves and for others, by clinging to these categories excessively for self-regarding reasons. As discussed earlier, this is the root of our tendency to relate to others in terms of "us" and "them." So cultivating greater equanimity with respect to others is extremely helpful, especially as an aid to living an ethical life.

To do this, you once again begin by relaxing and settling the mind through a breathing exercise and then proceed as follows. Call up an image of a small group of people you like, such as some of your close friends and relatives. Establish this image in as much detail and with as much verisimilitude as you can. Then add an image next to it of a group of people toward whom you feel indifferent, such as people you see at work or out shopping but do not know well. Again, try to make this image as real and detailed as possible. Finally, call up a third image, this one of a group of people you dislike, or with whom you are in conflict, or whose views you strongly disagree with, and again establish it as clearly and in as much detail as you can.

Having created images of these three groups of people in your mind, you then allow your normal reactions toward them to arise. Notice your thoughts and feelings toward each group in turn. You will find that your natural tendency is to feel attachment toward the first, indifference toward the second, and hostility toward the third. Recognizing this, you next turn to examining your own mind and considering how each of these three responses affects you. You will find that your feelings toward members of the first group are pleasurable, inspiring a certain confidence and strength coupled with a desire to alleviate or prevent their suffering. Toward the second group, you will notice that your feelings do not excite you or inspire any particular thoughts of concern at all. Toward the third group, however, the feelings you have will excite your mind in negative directions.

The next step is to engage in contemplation, using your critical faculty. The people we consider our enemies today may not remain so, and this is also true of our friends. Furthermore, sometimes our feelings toward friends, such as attachment, can lead to problems for us, while sometimes our interactions with enemies can benefit us, perhaps by making us stronger and more alert. Contemplating such complexities can lead you to reflect on the futility of relating to others in an extreme manner—whether they are members of the third group or even the first. Once you see that this way of relating to others impedes your ability to develop good will toward them and has a negative impact on your peace of mind, you then try to lessen the strength of your extreme feelings. Over time, the aim is to be able to relate to others, not as friends or foes according to your divisive classification of them, but as fellow human beings whose fundamental equality with yourself you recognize.

As for the second form of equanimity practice, many of the points already discussed in Chapter 2, the chapter on our common humanity, can be brought into our mental cultivation here. The key points are two simple truths: that just as I myself have an instinctive and legitimate desire to be happy and to avoid suffering, so do all other people; and that just as I have the right to fulfill these innate aspirations, so do they. Reflecting on these points, we can then ask ourselves, On what grounds do we discriminate so powerfully between ourselves and others? If we repeat this exercise over and over, not just in one or two practice sessions but over the course of weeks, months, and even years, we will gradually find that we are able to generate true inner equanimity based on a profound recognition of humanity's shared, innate aspiration to happiness and dislike of suffering.

REJOICING IN THE EXAMPLE OF OTHERS

Another exercise which can be very helpful in cultivating beneficial states of mind is a discursive practice taking as its object the good example of a person we greatly admire. This is similar, in some ways, to using role models as a means of inspiring ourselves. For those coming from a secular background, this can be someone past or present whom we especially admire for his or her compassion and selflessness: perhaps a doctor, a nurse, a teacher, or a scientist. For those of religious faith, it might be the founder of our religious tradition or some saint from its history. By reflecting on the admired person's life, contemplating how he or she lives or lived for others, how his or her behavior is or was characterized by compassion, we familiarize ourselves with their example.

One of the aims of this type of analytic mental training is to gain a direct appreciation of a given quality. In this case, we analyze what motivates people to devote themselves to others. Having identified this quality, we then focus on it, and rest our minds on it, as a way to unite ourselves with the quality through direct, intuitive insight into the compassionate motivation that is the ultimate object of this exercise. In other words, the idea is to train ourselves to act, in our daily lives, as the person we admire would act, so that when, for example, we become aware of others' suffering, we feel disposed to respond as this person would respond. We are thus seeking first to change our attitude toward others and then to change our behavior. This, after all, is the whole point of our practice: to inform and affect our actions. If it does not, then there is not much point in it.

DEALING WITH AFFLICTIVE ATTITUDES AND EMOTIONS

One area where discursive or analytic mental training can be highly effective is in dealing with destructive emotions and attitudes. A good place to start is by choosing an afflictive mental state that is dominant for you personally. All of us possess the entire range of afflictions, but individuals differ in the predominance of the specific types of afflictions. Some of us are more prone to afflictive emotions of the anger family, such as irritation, agitation, hostility, and temper. Others are more prone to envy, jealousy, and intolerance of other people's success, or to afflictions of the attachment family, such as desire, craving, greed, or lust. Some individuals have the opposite problem, namely that of indifference or inability to connect with others.

Having chosen which afflictive emotion or attitude you will address first, you begin as described earlier, relaxing the mind with a breathing exercise. Then you are ready to start the actual practice.

First, reflect on the destructive effects of the mental state you have selected. For anger, for example, reflect on the way it immediately disrupts your mental composure, the way it creates a negative mood and spoils the atmosphere around you. Consider, too, that in the heat of anger you have a tendency to say harsh things, even to those you care for deeply, and that, in general, it negatively affects your interactions with others. This contemplation of the destructive nature of these mental states needs to be sufficiently deep that over time your basic stance toward such states becomes one of caution and vigilance. A famous

Tibetan meditator once said, "I have only one task at hand: to stand guard at the entrance of my mind. When the afflictions are at the ready, I remain at the ready; when they stand easy, I stand easy."

Once you are convinced of the destructive nature of these afflictions, you then move on to the next stage of meditation. This involves developing a greater awareness of the mental states themselves, particularly of their onset. By becoming familiar with the way you feel when these emotions arise—how they feel physically in your body; how they feel subjectively or psychologically—you can learn to recognize them before they start to wreak their havoc. The more accurately you are able to identify the specific characteristics associated with the arising of specific emotions, the greater your chance to bring mindful awareness into the process and thus intervene early in the chain of causation.

The third stage of this mental cultivation practice for dealing with afflictive mental states is to apply the relevant antidotes to them: for example, forbearance to counter anger, loving-kindness to counter hatred, contemplation of an object's imperfections to counter greed or craving for that object. This can be enormously effective in causing afflictive mental states to subside.

In all three stages of this practice it is important, as suggested earlier, to combine discursive, analytic processes with resting your mind in single-pointed absorption on the concluding points. This combination allows the effects of your practice to seep deeply into your mind so that it begins to have a real impact in your everyday life.

Obstacles to Good Mental Cultivation Practice

It is only to be expected that to begin with the practitioner of these kinds of mental discipline will experience many trials and difficulties along the way. There are few worthwhile skills that can be achieved without a good deal of effort expended over a long period of time. In mental cultivation the challenge is even greater, since not only is the goal of our endeavor mental, but both the medium through which we practice and the domain in which the practice occurs are also mental. So even advanced practitioners encounter obstacles.

For everyone, whether beginner or expert, in addition to the general problems related to motivation, there are two principal obstacles to good practice. One is distraction, while the other is laxity or what we can call "mental sinking." A beginner is likely to experience distraction first: the scattering of the mind as it chases after thoughts, ideas, or feelings which keep it in an excited or agitated state and prevent it from reaching stability. Distraction may take the form of coarse excitement in which the object of our practice gets lost altogether. Or it may take a more subtle form in which, although the object is not entirely lost, a corner of the mind remains preoccupied with something else, preventing us from attaining proper focus.

How we overcome these obstacles to good practice depends on our individual experience. Sometimes it will be enough to recollect our purpose in undertaking this mental cultivation. At other times, we may have to leave off whatever we are trying to practice and move on to some other exercise. Or we may do a short breathing exercise, or repeat a few words suitable to the occasion. This may be as simple as saying, "I let go of my distraction," slowly and deliberately a few times. But sometimes we may need to break off the session and walk around the room for a few minutes. As usual, the important thing is not to become discouraged.

The other major obstacle to successful practice, laxity or mental sinking, is what happens when the mind becomes too relaxed. We succeed in withdrawing from our habitual preoccupations and manage to free the mind from distractions, but then, because our energy is low or we are not alert enough, the mind sinks and we become, as it were, "spaced out." These mental training exercises can be relaxing, but relaxation, in itself, is not the point of them at all. We need to cultivate and maintain a state of mind that is settled yet possesses alertness. In fact, prolonged habituation to a state that is relaxed but lacking in alertness can dull the sharpness of our minds.

How we overcome laxity will vary from person to person and from session to session. A short, brisk walk may be an effective remedy, or a few moments spent visualizing a bright light. For those with religious inclinations, briefly considering the surpassing qualities of some figure in their religious tradition may help. Another remedy is to imagine our consciousness springing up into space. Again, it is a question of whatever works best for the individual. In brief, if you find that your mind is a bit too downcast, this is an indication that the obstacle of laxity is beginning to surface. To counter this, you need to find a way of lifting up and activating the state of your mind.

The Question of Progress

In mental cultivation practice, as in any human activity, different individuals progress at different rates and reach various levels of accomplishment at different times according to their age, physical condition, intellect, and other factors. Some whose powers of introspection are powerful will quickly learn to spot the onset of either distraction or laxity and take measures to prevent the full development of either. Others will take longer to do so. In either case, this should not be a cause of either pride or sorrow. Instead, whenever obstacles arise, we should maintain an attitude of humility and seek to overcome them without anger.

The Joy of Mental Training

As we become more accomplished in our practice, we come more and more to see the trainability of the mind. We learn to substitute positive thoughts and feelings for negative ones and to weaken the hold that afflictive thoughts and emotions have over our minds. It is important, however, to be clear that what we are talking about here is not *suppressing* negative thoughts and emotions. Instead, we must learn to recognize them for what they are and replace them with more positive states of mind. And we do this not only to achieve self-mastery but also because attaining this kind of control over our minds puts us in a much better position to compassionately benefit others.

It is also important to bear in mind that we should never force ourselves to practice. As noted earlier, beginners will inevitably experience many distractions. It takes time to accustom the mind to the discipline of formal meditation practice. It is therefore essential to remain patient and not to become discouraged. If we find ourselves having to struggle, this can be a sign that it is time to break off the session. Trying to continue under such circumstances will not be effective. The more we struggle, the more exhausted the mind becomes. If we carry on under these circumstances, we will soon begin to dislike practicing. Eventually, even the sight of the place where we conduct our practice may cause feelings of revulsion. So it is important not to reach this point. Mental cultivation is about mental discipline, yes, but it is not meant to be a punishment. On the contrary, it is something to be enjoyed. We should try to take delight in our practice. When we succeed in doing so, our joy helps us to progress more quickly.

Impact on Daily Life

When we encounter problems in our daily lives, as all of us do from time to time, the practice of mental awareness can help us gain a more realistic perspective on what is causing us difficulty. If, for example, we exchange harsh words with someone—a family member, a work colleague, or a complete stranger—it is good to spend a few minutes during our practice holding the incident in our mind and inspecting our reactions to it. Then, visualizing our adversary in front of us, we try to generate feelings of gratitude toward him or her. This may sound strange at first. As I have already suggested, however, our enemies are, in an important sense, actually our greatest teachers, so these feelings of gratitude are in fact entirely appropriate. With this thought in mind, we visualize ourselves bowing down to our adversary. As we do this over and over, if our attitude is correct and our motivation pure, the aversion we feel toward this person will gradually dissipate and we will be able to generate compassionate love in its place.

Essentially, the purpose of the mental training exercises that I have been describing is, especially from the perspective of secular ethics, to make ourselves calmer, more compassionate, and more discerning human beings. But there are also other ways in which it can benefit us in our daily lives. In particular, as we progress, we create a degree of stability in our mind so that it becomes less prone to either overexcitement or depression; thus our practice helps protect us from the stress of experiencing too acutely the ups and downs of life. This is not to say that it anesthetizes the mind. What I am talking about is curbing intemperance. Mental training does not prevent us from experiencing life to the full, but it helps us to be more moderate in our responses. This may sound like a recipe for a boring existence, but if we reflect for a moment, we can see that having a mind which is like a small boat being tossed this way and that on a wild sea is not a very satisfactory state of affairs. Similarly, it is not helpful if the light in our room is one moment so bright that we can hardly see anything, and the next so dark that we can see nothing at all. What we want is a moderate, steady light which enables us to see the objects around us clearly. Thus when we develop some degree of control over our minds we are more able to take events, whether they are positive or negative, in our stride.

Just as I am not talking about anesthetizing the mind, neither am I talking about gaining complete mastery over the afflictive emotions. To do that takes a great deal of effort over a great deal of time. Rather, I am talking about the more modest goal of achieving a kind of habitual groundedness. Such a state is characterized by a natural humility and a robust peace of mind. These qualities in turn make the mind more manageable in our quest to develop compassion.

To conclude: in mental cultivation practice, moderate effort over a long period is the key to success. We bring failure upon ourselves by working overly hard or by attempting too much at the beginning. Doing this makes it highly likely that we will simply give up after just a short while. What good practice really requires is a constant stream of effort: a sustained, persistent approach based on long-term commitment. For this reason, practicing properly, even for a short period of time, is the best way. The emphasis should be on quality rather than quantity. And, above all, we should remember that the whole purpose of our practice is to become more compassionate human beings.

Afterword

In this book I have attempted to outline what I consider to be the key elements of a purely secular approach to ethics and to promoting basic human values. It is a project I have been committed to since I came to see that no one religion can ever hope to satisfy everyone. There are just too many differing mental dispositions among the seven billion inhabitants of our planet for that to be the case.

My motivation in undertaking this work reflects my firm belief that when each of us learns to appreciate the critical importance of ethics and makes inner values like compassion and patience an integral part of our basic outlook on life, the effects will be far-reaching. As I hope I have shown, at the level of the individual, doing so will help bring about greater happiness and provide a real sense of purpose and meaning in our lives. And at the level of society, as more and more of us do the same, there is a real chance that we will move decisively in the direction of a culture that is less materially focused and instead pays closer attention to our inner, spiritual resources. The benefits of doing so will be shared by all.

I am often asked whether I am optimistic for the future of humanity. My simple answer is yes. In the early part of the twentieth century, for example, it was widely believed that the solution to any serious conflict would have to come through the use of force. Happily, this view is no longer widespread. Today, people everywhere are fed up with war and genuinely wish to seek nonviolent ways to resolve differences. Similarly, until quite recently science and spirituality were widely considered to be incompatible, yet today, as advances in science penetrate ever more deeply into the nature of reality, there is growing recognition that these two domains of human endeavor can and in fact do complement one another. While in the recent past not many were aware of the impact of human behavior on the environment, today it is almost universally accepted that we need to be sensitive to the environmental impact of our actions, especially when it comes to economic development. And finally, while nationalism based on strong attachment to one's own country was a dominant force until quite late in the twentieth century, today, thanks to our increasing interconnectedness owing to communications and mass migration, its appeal is greatly diminished. As a result, the oneness and the interdependence of humanity are increasingly taken for granted. These are some of the reasons for my optimism.

In addition, I have always been a believer in the power of the individual. Throughout human history, many of the great developments that have helped change the course of humanity have emerged through the initiative of individuals. And each of these initiatives began with a vision and a belief in a new and better world. Whether it was William Wilberforce's campaign to abolish the slave trade, Mahatma Gandhi's nonviolent freedom movement in India, Martin Luther King Jr.'s civil rights movement, or my fellow Nobel Peace Prize laureate Jody Williams's campaign for the banning of antipersonnel land mines, in each case the inspiration came from individuals. It is likewise collections of individuals who, in supporting each of these campaigns, have helped bring about lasting change. Since society itself is nothing but a collection of individuals, human beings just like you and me, it follows that if we want to change society, it is up to each one of us to make our contribution.

Members of my generation belong to the twentieth century, which has already gone past. During that century, we humans experimented with many kinds of things, including large-scale war. As a result of the terrible suffering this caused, we have, I feel, become a little more mature, a little wiser. In that century we also achieved a great deal in terms of material progress. But in so doing we created social inequity and environmental degradation, both of which we now have to deal with. It is now down to the youth of today to make a better world than the one which has been bequeathed to them. Much rests upon their shoulders.

Given this fact, and also the truth that effective societal change can only come about through the efforts of individuals, a key part of our strategy for dealing with these problems must be the education of the next generation. This is one reason why, during my travels, I always try to reach out to young people and spend some time with them. My hope and wish is that, one day, formal education will pay attention to what I call education of the heart. Just as we take for granted the need to acquire proficiency in the basic academic subjects, I am hopeful that a time will come when we can take it for granted that children will learn, as part of their school curriculum, the indispensability of inner values such as love, compassion, justice, and forgiveness.

I look forward to a day when children, as a result of integrating the principles of nonviolence and peaceful conflict resolution at school, will be more aware of their feelings and emotions and feel a greater sense of responsibility both toward themselves and toward the wider world. Wouldn't that be wonderful?

To bring about this better world, therefore, let us all, old and young—not as members of this nation or that nation, not as members of this faith or that faith, but simply as individual members of this great human family of seven billion—strive together with vision, with courage, and with optimism. This is my humble plea.

Within the scale of the life of the cosmos, a human life is no more than a tiny blip. Each one of us is a visitor to this planet, a guest, who has only a finite time to stay. What greater folly could there be than to spend this short time lonely, unhappy, and in conflict with our fellow visitors? Far better, surely, to use our short time in pursuing a meaningful life, enriched by a sense of connection with and service toward others.

So far, of the twenty-first century, just over a decade has gone; the major part of it is yet to come. It is my hope that this will be a century of peace, a century of dialogue—a century when a more caring, responsible, and compassionate humanity will emerge. This is my prayer as well.